BADASS COOKERY
& GENERAL SHENANIGANS

KEVIN PAGENKOP

Badass Cookery & General Shenanigans

Published by Badass Books
www.BadassCookery.com

The cover design, logo, photos, and editorial work for this book are entirely the product of the author. The title font is 'Nexa Rust Sans Black 2', designed by Fontfabric™

ISBN (paperback): 9781662908064

TABLE O' CONTENTS

FIND YOUR FOOD...

I DON'T LIKE COOKBOOKS

I once sprained my ankle trying to jump into a pair of pants with both of my legs at the same time.

When I was a kid, during one of my precocious, prima donna moments, my mom tried to tether me back to reality by explaining that everyone gets into their pants "one leg at a time". Proved her wrong by getting tangled up in a pair of cranberry-colored corduroys and falling on my ass. I've always liked being different, pushing the boundaries, trying new things. Recipes always seemed restrictive. Too structured. Before committing to writing this book, I had never written a recipe down. I preferred to dig through the back of the fridge, clean out the pantry, and see what I could create with whatever was on-hand and whatever crazy ideas manifested in my head. My level of income and lack of any quality cooking equipment did not damper the enjoyment that came from "winging it". From being creative. From making something delicious out of scraps and leftovers. I learned that even though there were cookbooks telling you that you had to spend a chunk of cash on a mandolin to ensure that your veggies were cut to identical widths; or that 80% of your dinner budget needed to be dedicated to fresh, organic herbs imported from the Mediterranean; or that if you sautéed an item for 8-10 minutes instead of 6-8 minutes your meal would be ruined; that it was all bullshit. This is one of the reasons why people don't like cooking. Cookbooks are intimidating.

This isn't a cookbook. It's a playbook. A map. A list of parts that build an engine. (insert your favorite analogy here). Add your own unique tastes, creativity, and favorite ingredients, and have fun. Be fearless. The best recipes I have are because of mistakes that were made that wound up tasting good.

Is anyone actually reading this? I usually skip the preface of books. Who needs to listen to the author drone on about themselves? Blah, blah, blah. Boring.

In 1969 Johnny Cash recorded a live album at San Quentin prison. Riffing with the audience between songs he asks someone offstage to get him his red notebook which was in a briefcase. *"That briefcase back there of mine – ya know, that's got all the songs I stole in it."* He was tellin' it like it was. Most cookbooks are filled with familiar dishes and similar recipes. This isn't something to disparage, but rather, to encourage. By taking a family recipe, or being inspired by a meal prepared by a friend, or a dish eaten at a restaurant, and then adding your own twist and ideas, this is how recipes evolve. It's Culinary Darwinism.

The last few years have seen a movement toward gluten free, organic, and "super" foods like kale, acai, and blended wheat grass. Admirable. Not knocking progress but I'm a football watching, gun shooting, mid-western, badass. I love bacon, butter, red meat, BBQ, and grain alcohol. This is not a book for the faint of heart or easily offended. This is an old-school, grandma's lard recipes, cook with beer, as you drink beer, cookbook. Don't worry about counting calories, arterial plaque, or being politically correct. Food is culture. Food is history. Food is fun.

LIES!

I've never really used cookbooks. I found them filled with lies. 'Prep Time', 'Cook Time' and the list of 'Ingredients' – all lies. The Prep Time listed on many recipes are beyond human ability: "Peel 100 potatoes. 2 minutes." "Dice 2 onions, 3 stalks of celery, and 4 carrots. 1 minute." It's the same for Cook Times. They rarely take into account the thickness of the meat or the level of heat being applied: "Grill the steak for exactly 213 seconds per side". If I'd follow this direction with my King Cut Porterhouse then the inside would be so raw that my steak would "moo" when I cut into it. Or when a recipe tries to navigate around this by providing a range of cook-times: "Bake the salmon for 5-20 minutes". Far from helpful. Lastly, some of the ingredients listed on recipes require such an excessive investment of time when a can or jar of pre-made product would work just as well and without the hassle that accompanies words like "authentic" or "homemade".

PREP TIMES

There are no estimated 'Prep Times' in this book. Prep takes as long as it takes. And it shouldn't be a chore – prep is my Zen. I enjoy the repetition of julienne, the focus it takes to filet, and the de-stressing chop, chop, chop of dicing an onion and crying over my cutting board. It's a great way to transition from Work to Home. It's also a great way to get your dinner guests or family involved. Make Prep a group activity and give everyone a specific task. Kids make great Line Chefs.

COOK TIMES

What's the difference between Medium Heat and High Heat on a gas stovetop? Or an electric stovetop? Or a propane grill? These variances are going to impact cooking times. How do you know how long to cook for? – You don't. You approximate, experiment, and then make adjustments the next time you work the dish up. So consider these recipes as "general guidelines" and not "definitive instructions".

INGREDIENTS

I love cooking. And I love cooking from scratch as much as possible. But I also have a mortgage and bills. So there's this thing I do every week called "Go To Work". For those of you that have heard of this, you know that it pretty much sucks. So after a long day of playing "Go To Work", when I come home, I rarely have the time to invest 3-4 hours simmering 20+ ingredients into a proper Sicilian Gravy. As much as possible, I have included shortcuts for the recipes that follow. If a jar of pasta sauce, pre-diced veggies, or

spice mixes & sauce packets can be substituted to make your life easier, then that's just more time you have to enjoy the meal, your family, or knocking down the movies you have saved in your streaming queue.

MYTHS

1 You have to spend a lot of money and use the best ingredients for your food to taste good.
I've survived my whole life on dried spices, pantry staples, and leftovers – and never had an issue with the food not tasting dee-lish-ous.

2 You should be able to tell how done a steak is by pushing on it with your finger.
If you work in a restaurant and turn out dozens of steaks every night, and then the next night, and then twice that many on Friday night, then you're probably the master of the touch-test. If you're cooking at home for you and your family, use a meat thermometer. They are not that expensive and will save you a ton of guesswork and grief.

3 Measurements have to be exact.
This is why I'm not a baker. Cooking, as opposed to baking, is more forgiving. If you like a particular ingredient, use more of it. Don't like an ingredient, leave it out or replace it with something different.

4 You have to have a lot of kitchenware and expensive pots and pans.
While this certainly helps, it's not a deal breaker. Provided you have a pot, a pan, and a knife, you can cook. And if you like cooking, and this is something you want to spend your hard-earned money on, then build your collection over time (or encourage your friends and family to focus on specific items for your birthday and other gift-giving holidays. Nothing says "Happy Arbor Day!" like a 20" cast-iron skillet).

Notes on Knives

This is not a manual on knife skills. These recipes will still be delicious if you dice in place of julienne. Or if your slices are not mathematically even to the hundredth of an inch. Or if you shred in place of mince. And don't lose any sleep if you don't have a micro-plane, a deboning knife; or a Bluetooth, voice-operated, peppermill. Use what you have. If you want to develop your knife skills, that's great. The more even your cuts are, the more consistent the cook on your product. My culinary skills started woefully weak (one chef used the word "laughable" over a ham-incident that I'm still embarrassed about) but they developed over time the more I cooked. Cooking should be fun so don't get stressed-out over the recommended cuts or the specific knives you should be using. Regardless of what knife or knives you are using, make sure they are sharp. They don't have to be Hattori Hanzo sharp, but a dull knife is always more dangerous as you have to apply more force to cut and this often leads to the ol' slip & bleed.

SERVING SIZES

Why is the current culinary culture of this country geared towards massive-sized food and ginormous meals? The focus has been on quantity over quality. I get the concept of value, but I'm more in the adage-court of "you get what you pay for."

A cookbook that sketches out a recipe for 11-12 servings is only good for an NFL Starting Defense and would draw a flag if the additional DB didn't get out of the huddle and back on the sidelines before the ball was hiked. I'm not interested in doing Common Core Math to reduce a recipe by 5/6th so that it's fit for just my wife and I.

Most of the recipes that follow are for 2-4 servings. If you have a large family, are entertaining for friends, or just like having leftovers (delicious), then double/triple the recipes. It's easier to dial a recipe up than it is to knock it down. It's not that I don't like large portions – I just like variety. Have you ever been to a buffet? Do you put 6 servings of meatloaf on your plate and nothing else? I hope not. I'm assuming you mix it up and pile it high with meats, veggies, sides, and peel-and-eat shrimp. (If there isn't peel-and-eat shrimp, you're going to the wrong buffets.) So if you find a particular recipe is lacking in size, remember what Yoda said: *"one dish a meal does not make"*. These recipes are intended to be paired with other dishes and other recipes in this book. Just like Legos, you've got to build a great meal with lots of different pieces.

POLITICS

As human beings, the homo sapiens brain is hardwired to record its observations and then identify patterns. These patterns are then applied toward future behavior. So when you eat a raw jalapeno pepper, your brain remembers the pain associated with this action. The next time you see a jalapeno, your brain reminds you to steer clear. But the brain is flawed in that these patterns are only identified in our spheres of influence and can be distorted through the lens of our own perception. Consider: not everyone finds a jalapeno pepper hot; a cooked pepper is different than a raw pepper; jalapenos paired with other ingredients may taste different. The only way to ensure that your brain is evaluating complete data is to expand your range of experiences and observations.

As a kid growing up in the Midwest, restaurants were primarily steak & potato joints or burger shacks. How was I to know whether or not I liked Kimchi, Pierogi, or Shawarma? Unfortunately, fear drives a lot of our perceptions. What is foreign and unknown is scary. But America is the Great Melting Pot. The immigrants that built this nation, and continue to improve our country, have brought their cuisine and culture with them. This has provided more of an opportunity for exposure. And this exposure allows us to see that what once seemed different, is actually pretty similar.

Don't believe me? Have you ever had a calzone? Meat, vegetables, and cheese baked into dough. Basically, a pizza folded in half. Nothing too scary there. What do you think an Empanada is? Or a Samosa. Pupusa. Pierogi. Pot Stickers. Need I go on? Every culture has a version of meat or veggies packaged in a cooked dough. The only thing that makes these dishes something we're afraid of is our lack of exposure to them.

Thanks to the great inventions of television and the internet, these dishes, and cuisine from around the world, are brought into our homes and onto our mobile devices. "Sushi", "Tapas", and "Pho" are now in common parlance. Most cities now have more than one Thai Restaurant, representation from several different Central American Countries, and an opportunity to circle the foods of the Mediterranean clockwise from Gibraltar. We are fortunate that this exposure is helping to shape our perceptions for the better.

Use food to overcome your fears. The next time you're hungry – try something new.

INTRODUCTION

To help you navigate the following pages, raise your kitchen skills, and hopefully have more fun, the following icons are provided throughout:

 Tips and Tricks of the Trade. Turn your cook game up to 11.

 Kitchen Hacks. Shortcuts to save time and make cooking easier.

 Level Up. Recommendations to improve the recipes.

 Make-a-Meal. What to pair the recipe with to make it into a full meal.

 Link to Leftovers. Ideas for what to do with leftover ingredients.

XP: The Experience Points you'll be awarded for making each item.

Here's a few overall tips to help you get started:

Coarse ground Kosher salt is where it's at. The odd-shaped flakes adhere well to meat and help bring out that desired crust when searing over high heat. I also feel that the larger grains are easier to see so I have more control when trying to apply "a pinch". Unless otherwise noted, most of these recipes use a coarse-grain salt over standard table salt.

There are several different types of oil. When sautéing, use whatever oil you prefer. When making dressings, sauces, or just for dipping bread into, invest in a good olive oil. Olive oil should be Extra Virgin and First Cold Pressed. Which means it is thick and gold in color and not watery and yellow.

If you like garlic, and use a lot of it, buy minced garlic in a jar. In addition to saving the time it takes to peel, smash, and cut the fresh cloves, it will save you from having garlic-scented hands the rest of the night.

If you're not sure about spice level or saltiness, put less in. You can always add more at the end – but you can't take it out if it's too much.

Always pre-heat your pans. The times listed in these recipes assume that your pans are not Hoth-cold when you drop your food into them.

Heat is not a light switch. Whether the burners on your stovetop are electric or gas, take notice that they are not controlled by an 'On/Off' switch. If a recipe calls for Low Heat, then the burner should be set to its lowest setting. If you just crank the burner on without any thought to the Heat Level, say goodbye to any quality butter-based sauces. And the same holds true for searing. If the recipe calls for High Heat, you're not going to get anywhere if the burners are barely engaged.

Tips When you're cooking in your oven, especially when you're trying to make something crispy, place it on a wire rack over an aluminum-foil lined pan. Then it won't sit in its own rendered grease and the foil catches the drippings (to make clean-up easier).

Tips Make sure your meat is at room temperature before cooking. And when it's done cooking, let it rest before slicing into it or serving. Food continues to cook when removed from the heat. The temperatures indicated in this book are based on "carry-over cooking". Meaning: if you cook a chicken breast to the exact temperature you desire, the "carry-over" heat will push it from "done" to "overdone" (dry and gross). Removing the meat from the heat early accounts for "carry-over" and your meat will "rest" into the desired doneness.

Tips Butter is the nectar of the Gods. If you can, hook up an IV of melted butter and just lay back and let the fatness course through your veins. Butter based sauces are a great way to elevate your dishes but patience must be applied. Butter is both a fat and a liquid. When butter is heated over high heat, the fats and liquids separate and turn into a gross oily mess. But if the butter is gently warmed, stirred, and caressed like a new puppy, then your sauce will be velvety-smooth delicious. Follow the butter-sauce recipes closely for the best results.

Tips I've ruined too many recipes by salting a sauce to perfection, and then whisking in salted butter. Salted butter is my Kryptonite. All of the recipes in this book are built around unsalted butter. This allows you more control over the salt-level without getting surprised with your first bite.

Tips Clean up as you go. Why watch water boil when you can be cleaning your cutting boards and knives. Fill your sink with hot water and dish detergent. Then, as you cook, you can drop dirty dishes into the waiting sink. If they are greasy-nasty, let them sit. If they are just tasting spoons, dip, rinse, and drop in the drying rack so you can continue to use them. This makes cooking more fun as you don't have the dreaded after-feast clean-up.

Tips What is a tasting spoon you ask? The difference between a cook and a chef is the tasting spoon. You HAVE to taste as you go. More salt? More cheese? Taste, taste, taste. And if you are cooking for more than yourself, your dinner guests will appreciate the use of more than one spoon. Ya know, double dipping and all.

Tips Want to be a badass? Garnish. Chop some fresh parsley or scallions and sprinkle over the dish. Plate with lime wedges or lemon slices. Even a dusting of dried spice raises your presentation game. You could make a peanut butter and jelly sandwich, but if you sprinkle the plate with fresh rosemary and a dusting of paprika, you'll look like a pro.

USEFUL (AND UN-USEFUL) MEASUREMENTS:

1 Tablespoon (Tbs) = 3 teaspoons (tsp)
1 Ounce (oz) = 2 Tbs
1 Cup = 8 oz
1/8 Cup = 2 Tbs
1 gallon = 16 cups
1 tsp of minced garlic = 1 garlic clove
1 Tbs fresh parsley = 1 tsp dried parsley
1 lemon or lime = 2 Tbs of juice
Dash = 1/8 tsp
Pinch = 1/16 tsp
Smidgen = 1/32 tsp

1 Smoot = 5' 7"
My GCS before my morning coffee = 11
1 Parsec = 19 trillion miles
55 grain FMJ .223 = 3240 fps
Bugatti Chiron 0-60 mph = 2.3 seconds
1 carat = 200 milligrams
1 carrot = 61 grams
Carolina Reaper Chili Pepper = 2.2 million SHU
Lambeau Field = 81441 Seats
Depth of Lake Tahoe = 1,645 feet
1940 Macallan "M" = $631,850 USD per bottle

APPS

The meaning of this word sure has changed a lot over the last decade or two. Either way, the intention is to add excitement to our lives. And what's more exciting than bite-sized snacks or finger food? More times than not, if I'm at a restaurant I'm ordering off of the Appetizer or Starter Menu. Life is too short for me to waste my entire appetite on a single dish when I could order multiple smaller courses, line them up on the table, and just graze. This may seem gluttonous, but that is only because the portion sizes in this country are out of control like a cocktail meatball rolling down a hill and avalanching into a basketball sized meat-globe. (Look to tapas, botanas, and antipasto if you want to see how other cultures do this right.) Start downloading these Apps and get your grazing going.

FRENCH ONION SOUP SLIDERS

I don't love soup. Filling up on hot, flavored water before my Surf & Turf is served is unacceptable There are, however, exceptions. Gumbo, cioppino, pho, clam chowder in a sourdough bread bowl, and French Onion top the list. As the best part of French Onion Soup is the toasted bread covered in melting cheese, this recipe reprioritizes the ingredients in the best of ways.

• makes 4 sliders •

Accoutrements:
2 medium yellow onions
2 Tbs olive oil
2-3 Tbs unsalted butter
1 tsp coarse ground salt
1 1/3 cups of beef broth
    (10.5 oz can)
1 Tbs Worcestershire Sauce
1/4 cup white wine
    (I like chardonnay)
1 bay leaf
2 garlic cloves
8 slices of bread
1 cup shredded gruyere
    cheese (or 4 slices of Swiss)

1 Cut the ends off the onions and
remove and discard the first layers of peel. Slice into thin strips (1/4-inch thick).

2 Heat a large pan over Medium Heat and add enough olive oil to coat the bottom. Add 1 Tbs of unsalted butter. Once it's melted, add the onions. Simmer for 10 minutes, stirring occasionally. Add the salt and stir through. Reduce the heat to Low and cook for another 30 mins, stirring occasionally. Be patient. Cook the onions low and slow until they develop a beautiful tan.

3 Start making the dipping sauce by heating the beef broth in a saucepan over Medium-Low Heat. Add the Worcestershire Sauce, white wine, and bay leaf. Peel the garlic cloves and slice in half longways. Add to the pan and simmer for 25-30 mins to give everything a chance to take in some of that delicious wine.

4 Use a cup, bowl, or other circular object as a template to cut the bread into round slices. A 3-inch diameter works for a standard slice of bread. Brush the remaining butter on both sides of each piece of bread.

5 When the onions are done cooking, remove them from the pan and set aside. Turn the heat up to Medium-High and add the slices of bread to the pan. Brown the first side of bread until it is slightly toasty (about 2 mins). Flip and brown the second side (1-2 mins). Toast them in batches if necessary.

6 Spoon the onions (about 2 Tbs) onto half of the slices of bread. Top with a 1/4 cup of cheese (or one slice) and pop them under the broiler for 1-2 mins until the cheese becomes both ooey as well as gooey. Remove and add the remaining bread so the top half meets the bottom half of your sliders. Serve with the dipping sauce (with the bay leaf and garlic cloves removed).

FESTIVAL FARE MOZZ STIX

One of my first series of jobs was working at the many festivals that took place on the lakefront throughout the summer. The majority of the employees at the various food shacks and beer tents were all kids like me, working for minimum wage throughout the hot and humid festival season before we had to go back to school in the Fall. Trying to make the most out of this predicament, my crew of cohorts and I would engage in a bartering system of trading drinks for food on our breaks. Hopefully the statute of limitations has expired on this crime, but I'd swap plastic cups of brews for a handful of delicious Fried Mozzarella Sticks. Ahh, memories. Now that I'm grown, and way smarter, I realized that I can have both. So pour your favorite malted beverage into a plastic cup and follow this recipe so that you too can enjoy these delicious festival style Mozzarella Sticks.

• makes 8 •

Bartering Items:
wonton wrappers,
  egg roll size (6" x 6")
vegetable oil
1 egg
4 pieces String Cheese
  (mozzarella)
coarse ground Kosher Salt
dried parsley to garnish

1 Pour the vegetable oil into a pot - enough to fill it 2-3 inches. Heat over Medium Heat to a temperature of 350 degrees. It's going to take some time to come up to temperature so be patient. Resist the urge to turn the heat up as you don't want the oil Chernobyl-degrees Celsius.

2 Beat one egg in a small bowl and add an ice cube to keep it cold.

3 Cut each piece of cheese in half (should be 2 – 2 ½ inches long). Cheese should be at room temperature (this will help them fry-up and get melty).

4 Slice the wonton wrappers in half diagonally (into triangles). Place the cheese on the base end of the triangle and then fold each point in. Roll the cheese toward the tip. Brush a small amount of egg onto the tip of the wonton wrapper and finish rolling the cheese-stick. The egg will make it stick together while frying.

5 Once the oil comes to 350 degrees, gently slide in 2-4 cheese-sticks at a time. The quantity depends on how large your pot is. You don't want to add too many at once as it will drop the temperature of the oil and they won't be as crispy. Soggy cheese-sticks are pathetic cheese-sticks. And nobody wants sad, limp cheese-sticks.

6 Set a timer, or use the stopwatch on your phone, as these cook quick. Fry them for at least 2 mins and no more than 2 ½ mins. They should be golden brown and the cheese should just start bubbling out.

7 Remove and place on a wire rack to cool. Sprinkle with coarse ground salt and parsley while they are still hot. Serve with Marinara Sauce, or **Ranch Dipping Sauce**, or have some festival fun and serve with both.

(Tips) Wondering what to do with the leftover oil? Don't dump it down the sink. Let it cool and then pour it into a sealable jar. If the oil is relatively clean, you can reuse it. If it's discolored or has an odor, it's time to get rid of it. Some communities have drop-off locations where they collect grease and oil and recycle it. If you don't have that option, then discard the entire jar with your garbage.

Where do you get this jar? Recycle. Whenever you're done with a jar of olives, pasta sauce, pickles – save the jar. Then, when you need to dispose of cooking oil, you've got one handy and ready to go.

49ER BRIE & BREAD

I don't like the San Francisco 49ers. But I respect them. And in regards to NFL dynasties, respect must be given. Other than Coach Holmgren, this city by the Bay is also known for sourdough bread – and the invention of the bread bowl. Add some fancy-pantsy cheese to the game and you've got a championship dish that can be enjoyed as an appetizer or a meal in itself. So gooey-melty delicious it will make you want to wear a Dwight Clark jersey.

Draft Picks:
1 sourdough round (1/2 lb)
8 oz brie cheese
2-3 Tbs unsalted butter
garlic salt

1 Unless you are wearing a beret and eating a chocolate croissant in a Champs Elysée Café, remove the rind from your brie. The brie that you're going to find at your local market probably does not have a rind that's been matured long enough to be enjoyable. You won't contract mad cow disease if you leave the rind on, it will just melt better and have a smoother consistency without it.

2 In place of trying to make surgically-precise cuts between the rind and the cheese, use your knife as a scraper instead of as a slicer. Scrape the white rind off and you'll leave most of the cheese intact and unmolested.

3 Cut a circular section out of the bread, without pushing the knife to the bottom or out the other side. Use your hands to pull this section of bread out making sure that you leave a good thickness of bread at the bottom to retain the functionality of a bowl. Set aside the chunk you pull out – this will come in handy later.

4 Brush the inside of the bread with melted butter and season lightly with garlic-salt. Depending on the height of your bread bowl, make 2 to 3-inch slices down the sides, about an inch apart, without slicing down to the bottom or removing. These will be the "tear-away" pieces that you'll pull off and dip into the melted cheese after it is baked.

5 Slice the rind-less brie into 1-inch cubes and place them into your bread bowl. Bake at 385 degrees until the cheese melts into a smooth gooey-goodness (20-25 mins).

6 While this beast is baking, take the chunk of bread that you pulled out of the interior and slice into additional chunks that can, and absolutely should be, used to dunk into your brie-bread-bucket.

7 When the brie is baked and melty-delicious, plate it up and serve with the slices of bread and your favorite charcuterie snacks.

ROCKIN' RUMAKI

Who doesn't love a classic hors d'oeuvre from the 1960s? Cheesiness be damned, it's hard to beat bacon wrapped anything. Water chestnuts are a good point of entry for a delicious appetizer with few ingredients and minimal steps to make. Once you dial these in, level up your badassery by trying bacon-wrapped chicken livers, bacon blanketed portobello mushrooms, or bacon and shrimp. Rock on.

1 Soak the toothpicks in a bowl of water while you prepare the other ingredients.

2 Mix the hoisin sauce and soy sauce.

3 Add the whole water chestnuts and let them mingle with the sauce for at least 30 minutes to marinate.

4 Slice the strips of uncooked bacon in half. Wrap each water chestnut in a piece of bacon and fix it in place with a toothpick.

5 Place them on a wire rack (over a piece of aluminum foil or parchment paper to catch the drippings) and bake at 375 degrees for 25-28 minutes (until the bacon is crispy but before the sauce burns).

6 Remove from the oven and drizzle some of the remaining marinade over the top. Let cool for 5 minutes before serving. (Many recipes call for basting the bacon with the marinade halfway through the cook-time. Not a fan. I don't believe this extra step imparts that much additional flavor and the excess marinade usually just rolls off and burns to the bottom of the pan and sets the smoke alarm off.)

(K+) You can roll and toothpick these ahead of time and then just bake them to order.

• makes 20 •

Wrap Party:
20 toothpicks
1/2 cup hoisin sauce
2 Tbs soy sauce
1 (8 oz) can of water chestnuts (about 20)
1 lb bacon (10 pieces)

SRIRACHA DEVILED EGGS

The food tag "Deviled" was first used a few hundred years ago to refer to cuisine that was spicy. Makes perfect sense. Not sure how we got Deviled Eggs out of that because I've always found this dish boring; bland; and a last minute, thoughtless, pot-luck contribution of the unimaginative. Then I moved to Los Angeles and was introduced to "Rooster Sauce". This Vietnamese Sriracha Hot Chili Sauce was resurrected from an old Thai recipe from a city south of Bangkok called Si Racha. To honor this clever word play, I'm repurposing "Deviled" and spicing up these eggs with this delicious hot chili sauce.

• 6 eggs (12 servings) •

Etymology:
6 eggs
1/2 cup Japanese Mayo
2 tsp soy sauce
sriracha hot chili sauce

1   Place the eggs in a pot and cover with cold water until they are submerged at least an inch. Bring to a boil over Medium Heat. Once boiling, cover and turn off the heat. Let sit for 5-6 mins.

2   Mix the Japanese Mayo and the soy sauce together and set aside in the fridge. (Japanese Mayo is thicker and richer than traditional Western mayonnaise. You can use any mayo in a pinch, but once you try Japanese Mayo, you'll never switch back.)

3   Remove the eggs and place them into a large bowl filled with ice and water. Let the eggs sit in the ice water for 5 mins. This ice bath will "shock" them and stop them from overcooking. To make them easier to peel, remove them from their bath and let them come up to room temp.

4   Peel the eggs. If the shell sticks to the egg, or you pull chunks of the egg away with the shell, then you are a terrible cook and should throw everything out and start over. Or, on second thought, welcome to a not-so-exclusive club. I've found that the hardest thing to cook, seems to be an egg. But as long as they taste good, don't sweat the appearance.

5   Once peeled, slice the eggs in half lengthwise and gently remove the yolks without damaging the whites. The yolks should be yellow – not grey. If the yolk is grey then the eggs are over-cooked. Nothing you can do about this now, but you can reduce the "sitting time" for your next attempt.

6   Add all of the yolks to the mayo soy sauce mixture. Smash them with a fork to break up the chunks and then whisk everything together until it is smooth and creamy. Scoop a spoonful (about a Tbs) of the yolk mixture back into the egg-white halves. Finish by garnishing with a small drop of sriracha onto the top of each egg.

(Tips)   Fresher eggs seem to be harder to peel. This is a great recipe for when you have eggs in your fridge that have been there for a while and it's time to make some space for new groceries.

(K+)   Buy pre-boiled eggs. These can often be found in the cold deli section of your local market.

AUNT JO'S HOLIDAY SHRIMP DIP

Attending the first holiday dinner with your new boyfriend's or girlfriend's family is always an intimidating affair. In addition to the judgment of your worthiness as a mate, if you are bringing a dish, then it better dazzle them as this offering is going to add or detract from their overall impression of you. The first holiday I shared with Teri's family I couldn't tell you what I brought. It wasn't that I was overwhelmed meeting her

family, because her sister Jo was so warm and welcoming to me, it was because the focal point of the event was Jo's famous Shrimp Dip. Luckily, I'd picked the right family to marry into because this dip was a staple at every one of their family's holidays, birthday celebrations, and weekend BBQs. Now this is a tradition at *our* family's holidays, birthday celebrations, and weekend BBQs. I'm prone to meddling and enhancing recipes, but this one is so good (and easy) it requires no adjustments from the way she makes it. And also, I don't want to sleep on the couch.

Wedding Vows:
4 oz Bay Shrimp
  (also sold as "Salad Shrimp", frozen is okay)
8 oz cream cheese
12 oz sour cream
1/2 Tbs Worcestershire Sauce
1/2 Tbs hot sauce
1/2 tsp garlic powder
1/2 tsp table salt

1 If your shrimp is frozen, thaw in the fridge for a few hours (or overnight).

2 Let the cream cheese come to room temperature to soften up. Mix in the sour cream, Worcestershire Sauce, hot sauce, garlic powder, and table salt. Work any lumps out (because you deserve a velvety-smooth, cream-cheesey, shrimp dip).

3 Drain the shrimp but don't rinse it – you want the shrimpies to have a little delicious "shrimp love" remaining as this will further season the dip.

4 Add the shrimp to the dip and fold together. Let this party mingle in the fridge for at least an hour and then serve with your favorite potato chips, pita bread points, pretzels, or as I prefer it, shoveled straight into my mouth with a spoon.

GRANDMA LEONARDELLI'S OLIVA SCHIACCIATE

Who doesn't love olives? My very first time in a bar I ordered a martini (and yes, I ordered it "shaken, not stirred" – and with a straight face). After the bartender was done making fun of me, I realized that my palate was too young to enjoy the subtle intricacies of gin and vermouth – but those olives tho'. Other than growing up wanting to be a licensed "00" British Agent, the only other reason I continued to order and force-develop a taste for martinis, was because of my grandmother. No, she didn't work for MI-6 (as far as you know), but she was a fantastic cook and loved to do so for my brother and I. During the visits of my youth, we'd make olive salad together. It's one of my fondest memories and helped expose me to the delicious world of olives beyond the variety that's stuffed with a pimento and comes floating in a warm jar of brine.

1 There are several ways to remove the pits from the olives but I'm loyal to my grandmother's technique out of nostalgia. As kids, we'd get to help her pit the olives by using the bottom of a soda bottle. Yes, this is back in the olden days when sodas came in thick glass bottles. Pushing the bottom of the bottle down firmly on the olive will not only split the olive so that the pit can be easily removed, but it helps release the delicious oil. So crush the olives on a cutting board with raised edges so that the pitted olives can be scraped into a bowl along with all of the juices and oils crushed out of them.

Q Branch:
1/2 lb of your favorite whole olives
    (about 30 large olives)
    Avoid olives bought in a jar as these
    are pitted and brined (too soft to use)
2 garlic cloves, finely diced
1 cup diced celery
1/2 cup diced yellow onion
2 tsp dried oregano
1 Tbs red wine vinegar
1/2 cup extra virgin olive oil
lemon slices to garnish

2 Using your hands, remove the pits and discard. Depending on how big the olives are, tear them apart into 2-3 smaller pieces.

3 Dice the garlic, celery, and onions into small chunks. Add to the crushed olives.

4 Add the dried oregano to the vinegar and whisk as you slowly drizzle in the olive oil (use your A-List olive oil). Pour over the olives and veggies and marinate overnight to bring the flavors together.

This is also delicious on sandwiches - like a Muffaletta. If ya don't know, look it up 'cause you're missing out.

68ᵀᴴ STREET FRIED EGGPLANT

Getting takeout from the pizzeria of my youth included pizza, octopus salad, and french-fried eggplant. While the pizza fell under the culinary category of "freak'n awesome", it was the fried eggplant that I craved the most. And I hate vegetables. But these schnibles are so good that I have to dust off my Milwaukeese and speak in my native tongue, doe'n-ya-know. So da next time yer in da Cream City, get down to 'Tosa, aina hey. Pick up a large pie, a pint of Leinie's, and some fried eggplant once. Nostalgic as well as tasty? You betcha.

1 Slice each end off of the eggplant. Cut in half lengthwise and then into 1/2-inch thick slices. Lay the slices out and cut into 3/4 to 1-inch strips.

2 Spread the eggplant strips out on a cutting board or piece of parchment paper. Sprinkle both sides with salt. Let sit for 30 mins so the salt can pull some of the moisture out. After they sit for a while, place a handful at a time in a towel (or paper towel) and gently squeeze to remove more moisture. Repeat until all of the eggplant has been strained in this way. The drier the better.

3 Add the oil to a pot and start heating over Medium Heat.

4 Mix the two eggs in a bowl and add an ice cube to keep cold. Pour the flour into a large bowl. Dip a handful of the eggplant strips into the egg wash and then dredge through the flour. Shake off any excess and then set aside until all of the eggplant strips have been breaded.

5 When the oil heats up to 360 degrees, fry the eggplant in batches for 3-4 mins (until they are crispy-brown). Depending on the size of your pot and amount of oil determines how many strips you can fry at one time. Don't drop too many in or they will lower the temp of the oil and they'll come out soggy and sad. Ain't nobody got time for soggy eggplant.

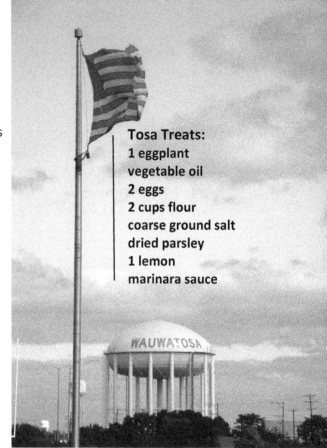

Tosa Treats:
1 eggplant
vegetable oil
2 eggs
2 cups flour
coarse ground salt
dried parsley
1 lemon
marinara sauce

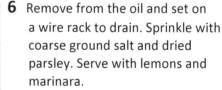

6 Remove from the oil and set on a wire rack to drain. Sprinkle with coarse ground salt and dried parsley. Serve with lemons and marinara.

(Tips) Keep the wire rack in an oven preheated to 250 degrees to keep the eggplant warm until you get through frying all of the batches.

SNACK TIME

The first time I was invited to a friend's house for a Holiday Dinner I was shocked to discover that the afternoon involved waiting around for the actual dinner. And when it was served, everyone sat down to eat – at a table. Weird, huh? My family's holidays involved having food out before the guests even arrived. We ate before, during, and after dinner. And snacks were always within an arm's reach of every seat (including (especially) the couch).

My dad taught my brother and I the hereditary tradition of valuing snacks, appetizers, and side dishes on the same level most families place upon the main course. We were introduced to at least a dozen different combinations of "cheese and crackers" by the time we were able to tie our own shoes. Our Uncle John, in addition to being the funniest person in the Universe (yes, bold claim), was the one who introduced us to the regional delicacy known as "summer sausage". And our grandfather was the master of all things smoked, brined, and cured. From smoked Lake Michigan Chub to Blue Cheese Stuffed Olives, it's clear that the patriarch of our family was keen on passing along his family's food traditions to his grandchildren. To make him proud, there are some nights when I pile each and every one of these treasured snacks onto a giant, hardwood cutting-board, shake up an ice-cold Martini, and call this culinary scrapbook "dinner".

Today, any restaurant with a wine list seems to offer snack plates like this but they call them "Charcuterie Boards" so they can charge you five times what they're worth. Take it from my family, it's more fun to put these together at home.

HERE'S A BRIEF TRANSLATION OF CHARCUTERIE TERMINOLOGY:

Hors d'oeuvres	=	snacky-snacks
Salumist	=	whomever picks the meats
Sommelier	=	the person that picks the wine
		(usually based on what the label on the bottle looks like)
Tapenade	=	mashed up olives that are too small to float in a martini
Pate	=	Liverwurst. Delicious liverwurst.
Brie	=	cheese wrapped in paper for some reason
Gruyere	=	Swiss cheese with 50% less holes that costs 50% more
Prosciutto	=	ham (sliced so thin you can see through it)
Prosecco	=	an Italian Sparkling Wine
Prosciutto-Prosecco	=	ham flavored sparkling wine (okay, I made this one up)
Baguette	=	bread that isn't sliced or full of Wonder
Artisanal	=	overpriced

Building a snack-plate or charcuterie-board is based on how many people will be sharing it and whether or not it will accompany a meal – or if it is intended as the entire meal.

Per Person:

	App	Meal
a Hard Cheese	2 oz	4 oz
a Soft Cheese	3 oz	6 oz
Meat #1	2 oz	4 oz
Meat #2	2 oz	4 oz
Olive #1	1 oz	2 oz
Olive #2	1 oz	2 oz
a dip	2 oz	4 oz
a bread		
some crackers		

Some Recommendations to Get You Started

Cheeses: Triple Cream Brie, Burrata, Saint Agur Blue, Port Wine Cheese, Humboldt Fog Goat Cheese, Asiago, Aged Gouda

Meats: Capicola, Finocchiona, Mettwurst, Summer Sausage, Hard Salami, Soppressata

Olives: Castelvetrano, Picholine, Cerignola, Dry-Cured Black Olives

Dip: Spinach & Artichoke, Artichoke-Parmesan, Crab Dip, Hummus, **Aunt Jo's Holiday Shrimp Dip**

 Apples, pears, mango, berries, pickled carrots, pickled green beans, pickled garlic, **Pickled Radishes**, mustard, olive oil & balsamic vinegar, artichoke hearts, sundried tomatoes, cornichon pickles, smoked salmon, anchovies, stuffed olives, pistachios, almonds, peanuts, cashews…

STELLA
ARTOIS

BELGIUM

Beer is
made from
Hops + healthy
Hops are
plants.

Beer = Salad

(you're
welcome)

GREEK SALAD

The Ancient Greeks are credited with inventing Theater, the Olympics, Philosophy, and Democracy. Of lesser importance to some, equal importance to others, they invented the Alarm Clock, Vending Machines, and Plumbing (and if you've ever eaten lunch out of a vending machine, you'll appreciate good plumbing). That's some pretty cool stuff the Greeks came up with and that was all the way back when we referred to the year with the abbreviation "BC". So when I heard that they also have a salad attributed to them...

• 4 servings as a side salad •
• 2 servings as a main (with chicken) •

Olympic Events:
1 head of lettuce, chopped
  (green leaf or red leaf)
1 large tomato
1/2 cucumber, peeled and chopped
15-20 kalamata olives, pitted
2-3 oz of feta cheese
Optional: cooked boneless/skinless
  chicken breast, sliced

Gold Medal Dressing:
1/4 cup olive oil (a really good one)
1/2 cup red wine vinegar
1 tsp Dijon style mustard
1 tsp lemon juice
1/2 tsp oregano
1/2 tsp basil
1/2 tsp garlic powder
1/2 tsp sugar
1/2 tsp table salt
1/4 tsp black pepper

1 For the delicious dressing, mix all of the ingredients except for your high-end extra-virgin olive oil. Whisk until the sugar is dissolved.

2 While whisking, slowly pour in the olive oil. Continue whisking until mixed. Set aside to give the flavors some time to get groovy together - at least an hour, more if you're able to plan ahead the night before.

3 Place the greens in a large bowl (if sharing family-style) or individual bowls. Layer the ingredients to your liking. Drizzle with the dressing and enjoy.

 Add diced avocado, heart of palm, marinated artichoke hearts, and/or red onion.

ROGUE SQUADRON SALAD BITES

After Wedge Antilles and Luke Skywalker blew up the Death Star, the second time, they returned to the rebel base on Endor and rocked out some of these delicious salad bites with Wicket and company while they sang "Nub Yub" over, and over, and over again. If you want to get your midichlorian count above 15,000, study the ways of these Salad Bite Appetizers. While they are no bigger than a womp rat, judge them not by their size. The Force is strong in Blue Cheese.

• 10-12 bites •

Rebel Alliance:
1/4 wedge of Iceberg Lettuce
3-4 strips of bacon (thick cut)
5-6 cherry tomatoes
1/4 cup of blue cheese crumbles
Blue Cheese Dressing

1 Cook the bacon and set it aside until it cools. Let me share a quick life-lesson: whenever you're making bacon – make extra. We both know that you're going to eat a piece (or two) before you're done with the recipe.

2 Cut the lettuce into small 1-inch cubes and slice the tomatoes in half. Cut the cooked bacon into 1 to 2-inch strips.

3 With a wooden skewer or toothpick, slowly twist a hole into the bacon, a wedge of lettuce, and then top with a cherry tomato. Sprinkle with Blue Cheese crumbles.

4 Serve with a side of **Blue Cheese Dressing** for dipping because you can never have too much blue cheese.

CAPRESE SALAD

This tricolore insalata delivers way more flavor than its list of ingredients would indicate. Based on the colors of the Italian Flag; basil, mozzarella, and tomatoes, are served with salted olive oil. Provided you can get fresh ingredients, this is a year-round favorite and is delicious with beef, poultry, pork, lamb, seafood, and unicorn. So pretty much everything.

1 Lay all of the basil leaves one on top of each other. Roll the leaves from tip to stem like a torcedor and then slice into 1/4 to 1/2-inch strips. Place in a bowl and sprinkle with coarse ground salt.

2 Use a super good olive oil (extra virgin, first cold pressed) and pour it over the top of the salted basil leaves. With the back of a spoon, press the salt and basil into the olive oil as you stir them together. This will help muddle the leaves so they give up their flavor and season the olive oil.

3 Slice the tomatoes and mozzarella balls in half.

4 Add the tomatoes and mozzarella to the basil and olive oil. Stir everything together.

⚠ Before serving, drizzle a good aged balsamic vinegar over the top. Aged = thick and sweet.

🔗 If you've got tomatoes left over, and you want to get the most out of them, make some **Rogue Squadron Salad Bites.**

• 2 servings •

Bandiera d'Italia:
8-10 Mozzarella Balls (Ciliegine or Bocconcini)
5-6 large, fresh basil leaves
8-10 cherry tomatoes
2 Tbs olive oil
1/2 tsp coarse ground salt
aged balsamic vinegar

ANTIPASTO PASTA SALAD

Meat? Check. Cheese? Check. Olives and artichoke hearts? Checkity-check! And then, double-down on the meat. And the cheese. And throw in some other goodies too. So even though this is called a salad, don't be fooled. This is a bowl of badassery. It works as an appetizer, a side dish, or as an entire meal.

Cast of Characters:
1 box (12-16 oz) of tri-color rotini pasta
3/4 cup extra virgin olive oil
1/4 cup balsamic vinegar
3 Tbs Italian Seasoning
Approximate: (make to your tastes)
    1/4 lb (4 oz) of each of the following:
        hard salami
        pepperoni
        mild cheddar cheese
        mozzarella cheese
    1 (6 oz) can of black olives (medium sized)
    8-10 Spanish Queen green olives (pitted)
    3-4 Roma tomatoes
    6 oz marinated artichoke hearts
coarse ground salt (to taste)

1   Whisk the olive oil, balsamic vinegar, and Italian Seasoning together. Set aside to give the flavors of the dressing some time to get to know each other.

2   Cook the pasta according to the package. When done, drain and run the pasta under cold water to shock it and stop it from cooking further. Set aside in a colander to drain and cool.

3   Cut the meat and cheese into 1/2-inch by 1/2-inch cubes. Slice the olives in half. Slice the ends off the tomatoes and then slice in half lengthwise. Scrape out the seeds and discard. Cut into 1/2-inch chunks.

4   Place the pasta in a large bowl. Re-whisk the dressing to wake it up and then pour over the top. Stir through to coat all of the pasta. Add the remaining ingredients and stir the party together. Let sit in the fridge for at least an hour for the dressing to work its magic. Salt as necessary.

MARKET DELI SEAFOOD SALAD

Sometimes the best things in life are actually easy. See food. Make food. Eat Food. Seafood. This grocery-market deli inspired salad can be whipped up quick, lasts a good long time in the fridge, and is begging to be your next side dish of choice when you host your next BBQ.

1 Cut the "crab" sticks into thirds and then pull or slice them apart to shred them.

2 In a bowl, mix the mayo, lemon juice, and lemon-pepper seasoning.

3 Stir in the thinly sliced celery and the shredded "crab".

4 Cut the avocado in half lengthwise and remove the skin and pit. Slice into strips and then dice (chunks about the size of a sugar cube). Fold the avocado into the mixture and let the salad sit in the fridge for at least an hour to let the flavors set. Salt to taste and serve with lemon.

Shopping List:
16 oz imitation crab (surimi)
2/3 cup mayo
juice of 1 lemon
1 tsp lemon-pepper seasoning
1 cup thinly sliced celery
1 avocado
salt to taste

 If you have leftover shrimp from any of the shrimp recipes, which would be odd because they are all uber-tasty-delicious, you can dice them up and add them to this salad as well.

ORZO PASTA SALAD

I don't like salads. You'll notice that the "salads" in this cookbook aren't really the salads most of us have grown up with (lettuce; quartered tomatoes; store bought, tooth-chipping, croutons; and a bottle of dressing that you found in the door of your fridge – unknown date of origin). But this "salad" is a vacation to the Mediterranean. It includes a collection of some of my favorite items, all thrown together in a bowl, and then tossed in extra virgin olive oil – so, basically, badass.

• 4-5 servings •

Gibraltar's Gifts:
1/2 a box of orzo pasta
10-12 kalamata olives
2-3 Roma tomatoes
5-6 basil leaves
4 Tbs extra virgin olive oil
1/2 Tbs coarse ground salt
3-4 oz feta cheese crumbles
2 ½ - 3 Tbs pine nuts

1 As the size of the ingredients can vary, and everyone has different tastes, there is a lot of customization that can, and should, occur with this recipe – add as much or as little of each ingredient to your liking.

2 The olive oil is the engine that drives this racecar. The majority of these ingredients are very affordable, so save up the extra money and splurge by buying a good olive oil.

(Tips) Look for "first cold pressed". This oil is thick and golden in color and brings a lot of flavor when you use it. The cheaper olive oils are bottled on the backend of production and are watery and clearer in color. If you don't believe me, buy both and do a taste test. But I'm tellin' ya, "first cold pressed, extra virgin" is the gangster-ninja of olive oils.

3 If the kalamata olives have pits, place them on a flat surface and gently push the bottom of a bottle (or the flat end of a large knife) down onto the olive to split it and pull the pit out. Slice into halves or quarters (depending on the size).

4 Cut off the end of each tomato. Slice lengthwise in half. Using a spoon or a small knife, scrape out the seeds and dump them. Chop into small chunks.

5 Remove the stems from 5-6 basil leaves and cut lengthwise into long strips.

6 Follow the directions on the pasta to cook half the box "al dente". This is enough for 4-5 servings. If you are cooking for more people, or you want leftovers (this salad keeps well in the fridge for several days), then cook the whole box of pasta – but don't forget to double the amount of the other ingredients too.

7 When the pasta is cooked, strain the water and pour the pasta into a large bowl. Add the olive oil and salt and stir through. This may seem like a lot of salt and olive oil, but it will be absorbed by the orzo (as intended) and the rest of the ingredients help balance the flavors.

8 Once the pasta reaches room temperature, add all of your other ingredients and stir them together.

 Try adding lemon-garlic grilled chicken breast (diced), marinated artichoke hearts, green olives, sundried tomatoes, red onions, or caramelized yellow onions. You can also take this to the next level by drizzling aged balsamic vinegar over the top prior to serving.

 For a fun plating option, and to get some "wow responses", serve the orzo salad in a halved and hollowed out bell pepper or large tomato.

HAWAIIAN MAC SALAD

Pa Mea'Ai. The Hawaiian Plate Lunch. Meat, rice, and a creamy macaroni salad that is delicious served warm or cold. This is an awesome side to more than just Island Food. Enjoy with BBQ, short ribs, Char Siu, grilled steak or veggies, or just in a bowl drizzled with some soy sauce.

Navigational Chart:
1/2 lb elbow macaroni (1/2 box)
1/4 cup diced green onions
1/4 cup apple cider vinegar
3/4 cup finely diced cooked ham
2/3 cup finely diced celery
1/4 cup shredded carrot
1 cup mayonnaise
1/4 cup milk
1/2 Tbs coarse ground salt
1 tsp white pepper

1 Cook 1/2 the box of elbow macaroni according to the package directions.

2 When done, drain and then add the macaroni back into the pot it was cooked in. While the pot and pasta are still warm, add the diced green onions (greens and whites) and the apple cider vinegar. Stir it all together for 2 mins until the hot macaroni has absorbed most of the vinegar. Set aside to cool.

3 Dice the ham into small cubes and finely dice the celery.

4 Shred the carrot with a cheese grater.

5 In a large bowl, mix the mayo, milk, salt, and white pepper. When the pasta is cool, pour it into the mayo mixture and stir thoroughly.

6 Fold in the ham, celery, and carrot. Let it all hang out in the fridge to allow the flavors to really come together. Overnight is best but you can serve in 4 hours if you've got a plane to Hawaii to catch or you're as impatient as I am.

(Tips) To maximize your time, take advantage of how long it takes to boil the pasta water and prepare the other ingredients.

22.051924, -159.327397

ICE

STEP ONE:

Start by travelling to Heathrow Airport. Rent a car and take the M4 to A40 to A3220 to Grosvenor Road. Use the Lambeth Bridge to cross the Thames River and head North to Lambeth Palace. Find the Archbishop of Canterbury and rent the spoon of antique forme. After you have the Coronation Spoon, make your way to the St. Pancras Train Station.

STEP TWO:

Buy a ticket on the Eurostar to Paris. I recommend Business Premier as it includes a hot meal and champagne.

STEP THREE:

After passing beneath the Strait of Dover and arriving in Paris, take A4 Autoroute de L'Est northeast to the city of Reims. In the Cathedral Notre-Dame de Reims, borrow the twelfth century Saint Remi Chalice. If you can't borrow it, you won't be able to buy it, so grab and run fast. Return to Paris and make your way to Charles De Gaulle Airport.

STEP FOUR:

Fly to Punta Arenas, Chili.
From there, purchase a flight to King George Island in Antarctica.
Once you get to Antarctica, book a C1 category vessel from the IAATO to sail to Goudier Island. After you arrive, take a rigid-hull inflatable boat and dock in Port Lockroy. Procure some snowshoes and a warm jacket and walk inland to make your way to the top of the glacier. At coordinates -64.8034662,-63.4173137 stop and fill the Chalice with the glacial snow.

STEP FIVE:

Return home. (Note: the glacial snow in the Chalice will melt by the time you get back.)

STEP SIX:

Place the St. Remy Chalice, filled with the melted Antarctic glacial snow, in your freezer. Every hour, use the Royal Coronation Spoon to gently stir the water in the center of the chalice to allow any remaining impurities or gases to escape as the ice solidifies from the outside in. The water should be completely frozen after twelve hours.

STEP SEVEN:

Remove the frozen block of water from the chalice. Using a lathe, slowly whittle down the ice into a 1" x 1" x 1" cube.

*Note: For more than one ice cube, repeat recipe from Step One.

CHICKEN

Teri loves chicken. And when your wife loves chicken, then you love chicken. This photo is where I proposed to her. And where we came back and got married.
And also home to a damn fine cup of coffee.

POUTINE CHICKEN SANDWICH

Canada is pretty sweet, eh. If it's your home and native land, then I assume you've been raised on poutine. Poutine, hockey, and Rush. But for your neighbors to the south, they need to get in on the brilliance that is French fries smothered in brown gravy and topped with melted cheese. (As well as the brilliance that is Geddy Lee.) So put on your tuque, drink a Molson, and make this sandwich, ya hoser.

1 Place boneless, skinless chicken breast in a plastic bag and seal tightly. With a meat tenderizer or a hockey stick (a goalie's stick works best), pound the chicken breast until it begins to spread out and get thinner. Cross-check each one of them into the boards until they are 1/4 to 1/2-inch thick cutlets.

2 Set out 3 bowls large enough to accommodate the chicken cutlets. In the 1st, add the flour and season with the garlic salt and black pepper. In the 2nd, beat the egg and add an ice cube to keep it cold. In the 3rd bowl, add the breadcrumbs. Skate down your assembly line of bowls and coat both sides of the chicken in the seasoned flour, then the egg, and lastly in the breadcrumbs.

3 Coat a pan in olive oil and wait 1-2 minutes for the oil to heat up. Cook the chicken 3-4 mins each side. While it's cooking, let the chicken sit without moving it around so that the hot pan can do its job and the cutlets develop a nice tan. When the internal temp is 160 degrees, remove and rest on a wire rack.

4 Slice the rolls open and place a cutlet into each one. Depending on the type and size of the roll, you may need to cut the chicken in half so it fits.

5 Cover in brown gravy. Use as much or as little as you prefer depending on how much you enjoy getting your hands dirty (and arms, face, shirt, the floor, pets).

6 Place a handful of cheese curds onto the top and shoot the sandwich under the broiler for 2-3 mins to melt the cheese. Pair with an ice-cold beverage and it's game time.

• recipe for 2 •

Power Play Unit:
3 chicken breasts,
boneless and skinless
1/2 cup flour
1/2 Tbs garlic salt
1/4 tsp black pepper
1 egg
1/2 cup breadcrumbs
olive oil
brown gravy
cheese curds
2 rolls

KEVIN'S CHICKEN

This chicken could be named after me because we're both smokey, hot, and sweet.
More plausibly, because it's traditional Jerk.

• 3-4 servings •

Junk for Jamaican Jerk:
1-4 habanero peppers
    (1 for medium hot, 2 for hot,
     3 for very hot, 4 for Jamaican)
1 bunch green onions (5-6 stalks)
Juice of 1 lime
1/4 cup white vinegar
1/4 cup orange juice
2 Tbs brown sugar
2 Tbs soy sauce
2 Tbs vegetable oil
1 Tbs allspice
1 Tbs minced garlic
1 tsp table salt
1 tsp thyme
1 tsp cinnamon
1/2 tsp nutmeg
1/2 tsp black pepper
4 pieces chicken
    (thighs and/or drumsticks)
3 Tbs unsalted butter, cold

1 Remove the stems from the habaneros. Be a badass and leave the seeds and veins in to get the full heat and flavor. Rough chop and add to a blender. Slice the tip off each green onion and then chop them into 3-4 pieces and add to the blender. Add all of the other ingredients (except the chicken and the butter) and blend until smooth.

2 Place the chicken in a large bowl or a sealable plastic bag and pour the blended marinade over the top. Marinate in the fridge for at least 4 hours (overnight is best).

3 Remove the chicken from the marinade (keep the sauce, set it aside for now) and place on a wire rack over an aluminum-lined baking sheet (to catch the drippings). Bake at 375 degrees for 35-40 minutes until the internal temp is 160 degrees.

4 While the chicken is in the oven getting happy, pour the remaining marinade into a saucepan and bring to a boil over Medium-Low Heat. Boil for 5 minutes and then turn off the heat. Add 3 Tbs of cold butter, 1 Tbs at a time, stirring non-stop until each one is melted.

5 When the chicken is done, serve with (or over) white rice. Depending on how much you like spicy food, sprinkle, drizzle, or pour the buttered marinade sauce over the top.

TI-MALICE HAITIAN HOT SAUCE

In Haitian folklore, the trickster character of Ti-Malice is routinely pranking his Uncle Bouki. After several occasions where Bouki happens to visit just when Ti-Malice is sitting down to eat dinner, and then greedily helps himself to the meal, Ti-Malice decides that he is going to make a sauce with the strongest and hottest ingredients before Bouki's next not-so-coincidental visit. He mixes onions, garlic, vinegar, limes, and the blazing hot Caribbean pepper – the Scotch Bonnet. The following night, just as he finishes preparing his dinner, Uncle Bouki arrives on cue as expected. Ti-Malice presents the sauce and convinces Bouki to pour it all over his meal. Waiting expectantly for Bouki's horrified reaction, he's shocked to find that Bouki loves the spicy-sweet hot sauce. While Ti-Malice's prank backfired, the sauce spread across the island and became one of the most popular condiments.

1 Remove the stems from the peppers and slice into small chunks. Dice the onion into small chunks.

2 Heat the oil in a saucepan or pot over Medium-Low heat. Add the peppers, diced onions, and salt, and sauté for 5-6 minutes.

3 Drop in the tomato paste, garlic, black pepper, and dried thyme. Stir until the tomato paste breaks down. Simmer for another 2-3 mins.

4 Add the lime juice, vinegar, and water. Turn the heat up to Medium-High and bring to a boil. Then reduce the heat to Low and simmer for 15 mins.

5 Let the sauce cool to room temperature and then blend until smooth. If you blend while the sauce is hot, make sure the lid is secured tightly, and you're holding it down with one hand, and you're blending on a very low setting. Seems like a lot of steps, but so is cleaning the sauce off of your kitchen ceiling when it explodes out of your blender.

• 20 ounces •

Prank List:
3 scotch bonnet peppers or habaneros
1/2 small onion, diced
2 Tbs vegetable oil
1 Tbs coarse ground salt
2 Tbs tomato paste
1 Tbs minced garlic
1/2 tsp black pepper
1/2 Tbs dried thyme
juice of 2 limes (1/4 cup)
1/2 cup apple cider vinegar
1 cup water

 As this sauce will last a few weeks in your fridge, pour it into a super cool bottle (like a Bourbon bottle) for that little bit of extra badassery.

TLC CHICKEN PICCATA

On one of the first dates my wife and I went out on, she took me to her favorite restaurant for chicken piccata. You'd think this would have been a recurring meal that I lovingly made for her weekly, but the chicken was so crispy fantastic and the velvety lemon sauce so decadent, it seemed beyond my skills in the kitchen. Not too smart of me as this dish is actually pretty easy to make. Guess my wife didn't marry me for my brains. Or my looks. Sense of humor? One out of three isn't bad.

• recipe for 2 •

Compatibility Profile:
3 boneless, skinless, chicken breasts
1/2 cup flour
1 Tbs flour
1/2 Tbs garlic salt
1/2 tsp black pepper
1 egg
1/2 cup breadcrumbs
3 Tbs unsalted butter (cold)
1/2 tsp minced garlic
1/4 tsp coarse ground salt
juice of 1 lemon
1 cup chicken stock
1 Tbs capers
6 oz mushrooms, sliced
olive oil

1 Place boneless, skinless chicken breasts in a plastic bag and seal tightly. With a meat tenderizer or a rolling pin (or any sturdy object), pound the chicken breasts until they begin to spread out and get thinner. Keep whacking until they are 1/4 to 1/2-inch thick cutlets.

2 Set out 3 bowls large enough to accommodate the chicken cutlets. In the first, add the 1/2 cup of flour and season with the garlic salt and 1/4 tsp of the black pepper. In the second bowl, beat the egg and add an ice cube to keep it cold. In the third bowl, add the breadcrumbs. Move down your assembly line of bowls and coat both sides of the chicken in the seasoned flour, then the egg, and lastly in the breadcrumbs.

3 Heat a large pan over Medium-High heat. Coat the bottom in olive oil and wait 1-2 minutes for the oil to come to temperature before laying the cutlets in. Cook the chicken 3-4 mins each side. While it's cooking, let the chicken sit without moving it around so that it can develop a crisp, golden crust. When the internal temp is 160 degrees, remove and let them rest on a wire rack.

47.542437, -121.837847

4 Turn the heat down to Medium. Add 1 Tbs of the butter and the minced garlic. As the butter melts, use a spoon to scrape up any chicken-bits of flavor that stayed behind in the pan. Add the remaining 1/4 tsp of black pepper, the salt, and the lemon juice. Stir and simmer for 2 mins. Whisk in the remaining 1 Tbs of flour and keep stirring to break up any lumps. Stir in the chicken stock and simmer until the sauce starts to thicken (5-6 mins).

5 Add the capers and mushrooms and cook for another 3-4 mins until the mushrooms soften. Turn the heat off. Stir in the remaining 2 Tbs of cold butter, 1 Tbs at a time, stirring constantly until they are melted.

6 Plate the chicken and spoon the creamy lemon-caper sauce over the top.

 Serve with pasta. Angel hair is nice and dainty and not too heavy of a starch.

 If you're going through the trouble of pounding out cutlets, breading them, and then frying them up, make extra. You can then make **Poutine Chicken Sandwiches**, or chicken parmesan, or just have another round of **TLC Chicken Piccata** the following night – it's twice as nice.

TINA'S CHAR SIU CHICKEN

If you have ever been to China, or a Chinatown, or a Chinese Restaurant, (or watched a movie set in one of these locations), you have no doubt seen poultry or pork barbequed to a beautiful, deep red color. I never knew that it was possible to make this at home until my super-cook daughter-in-law busted this out one night for us – and now this chicken is in our weekly rotation of favorite dinners. While this sauce is traditionally red in color, red fermented bean curd is not an ingredient that is easily found and I just can't get myself to buy red food coloring just to make this sauce look pretty. But if you're entertaining and want to go for the "wow factor", a couple drops of red food coloring will make this marinade look like traditional Char Siu Sauce. (or check out the hack below for pre-packaged dry marinade)

• 4 servings •

Cantonese Cupboard:
4-6 chicken thighs
1/4 cup hoisin sauce
1/4 cup soy sauce
1/4 cup honey
2 Tbs oyster sauce
2 Tbs mirin (rice wine)
2 tsp Chinese Five Spice Powder
2 tsp powdered garlic
1/2 tsp coarse ground salt
1/2 tsp white pepper
1/2 tsp powdered ginger
red food coloring (optional)

1 Mix all of the ingredients together except the chicken thighs. Whisk to get the honey incorporated.

2 Place the chicken in a bowl or sealable plastic bag and pour the marinade over the top. Marinate overnight (4 hour minimum).

3 When the chicken is done marinating, remove from the fridge and let it come to room temperature (about 20 mins).

4 Heat a grill to Medium-High Heat. Grill the chicken skin-side up, off heat (away from the flames), for 30-35 mins. If the grill gets too hot, or the chicken gets too close to the flames, the sauce will burn. When the internal temperature is 160 degrees, flip the chicken skin-side down and move over the heat for 3-4 minutes to crisp the skin (don't walk away as the skin can turn from tasty-crispy to Infiniti Stone charred Avenger very quickly).

If you are not able to grill, place the chicken on a wire rack over an aluminum foil lined baking sheet (to catch the drippings). Bake for 35-40 minutes at 375 degrees.

 If you can find it (or order it), buy the packaged version of this sauce. It's a red powder that is usually mixed with water to create the marinade. To make a thicker and tastier sauce, Tina's trick is to reduce the amount of water by half and add 1 Tbs of Oyster Sauce.

If you have leftovers, which is a big IF, remove the chicken from the bones and make **The World's* Best Chinese BBQ Tacos**.

THE WORLD'S* BEST CHINESE BBQ TACOS

Fusion. Hybrid. Cross-over. These are just cookbook clichés. All that we need to know about combining two different types of cuisines we learned in elementary school math. Tasty x Tasty = Tasty^2

• recipe for 3-4 •

Products to procure:
2 boneless, skinless chicken breasts
    (about 1 ½ inch thick)
Char Siu Sauce
1 large carrot
3 to 4-inch chunk of daikon
1 cucumber
8-10 small tortillas (I prefer flour)
cilantro (to garnish)

1 Marinate the chicken in Char Siu Sauce (see **Tina's Char Siu Chicken**) for a minimum of 4 hrs (overnight is best).

2 The garnish is a slaw of carrots, daikon, and cucumber. Peel the carrot and remove about 1/4-inch off each end.

 When cutting a round vegetable, carefully slice a thin strip off one side to create a flat base. It will then lie flat and not roll around as you cut it.

Make thin lengthwise slices down the carrot. Lay the slices flat, and slice them again into thin sticks. Lastly, cut them down to size to a length of 2 inches.

Peel the daikon and cut about 1/4-inch off each end and discard.
Slice into 2 inch sticks the same way you cut the carrot.

Remove the ends from the cucumber and slice lengthwise in half. Using a spoon, scrape out the seeds. Slice into thin strips, then sticks, and then down to 2 inches. Toss all the veggies together in one bowl.

3 After the chicken has marinated, let it come to room temperature (20 mins). Grill for 5 mins a side over Medium Heat. Keep the lid open to watch for flareups. Move off heat, close the lid, and cook until the internal temperature is 160 degrees (about 15 mins). When done, let rest for 5 mins and then cut into bite sized chunks.

4 Warm a large pan over Medium Heat. When warm, add the tortillas (as many at one time as you can, provided they don't overlap). Warm on each side for 1-2 mins until they get soft (not crispy).

5 To build the tacos, place the tortillas on a plate, add the chicken, and then top with the vegetable slaw. Garnish with fresh cilantro.

Try these tacos with **Pickled Onions.**

*Legal disclaimer: "The World" does not imply the entirety of plant Earth. It is "Kevin's world". Which includes a few isolated postal codes in a handful of American States, Middle Earth, the colony on LV-426, Klendathu, the asteroid Eros, Arrakis, Westeros, Asgard, and the Mos Eisley Cantina on Tatooine. It's been voted and designated 'The Best' in these worlds.

FOOD FACTS

How many different flavors of Froot Loops are there? If your answer is anything more than "one", you'd be wrong. While there are several different colors, all Froot Loops are flavored exactly the same. Also, take note that fruit is spelled "froot" as there is absolutely no fruit in this cereal.

The largest crab in the World is not the Alaskan King Crab but a species on the complete opposite side of the globe: the Tasmanian Giant Crab. It can weigh close to 40 pounds and the shell across its back can be 18 inches wide. The Japanese Spider Crab is a close second. While the body is slightly smaller, its leg-span can reach 12 feet, tip to tip.

French Fries are not French. Sliced and fried potatoes were invented in Belgium. They are only called French fries because the potatoes were sliced into a French cut.

Most ears of corn have 16 rows of kernels. Most oranges have 10 segments.

Arachibutyrophobia is an eighteen-letter word for people that have the fear of getting peanut butter stuck to the roof of their mouth.

The word "burrito" is a derivative of the Spanish word for donkey, "burro". These little donkeys, burritos, were named for a tortilla's ability to carry a lot of ingredients in the same way a donkey is used to carry goods.

During the medieval period, tomatoes were referred to as "poison apples". People were frequently getting sick, and many died, after eating them. It wasn't until years later when it was determined that the acidity in the tomatoes was reacting with the plates they were served on and people were getting sick from lead poisoning and not from the tomatoes.

In Norse mythology, half of the Vikings who die in battle are taken to Valhalla, a great hall in Asgard ruled by the god Odin. There they feast on an endless supply of bacon and beer. The pork is provided from the mythical Sæhrímnir – a boar that is butchered and cooked each evening only to be reincarnated the following day. If that wasn't badass enough, Heiðrún is a magical goat whose udders produce an endless supply of mead. (extra points if you can correctly pronounce these)

The World Record for the hottest pepper belongs to the Carolina Reaper. This variety of pepper was made by combining the La Soufriere Pepper and the Naga Viper Pepper and can exceed 2,000,000 heat units on the Scoville Scale. For comparison, a Jalapeno Pepper is only 3,000 Scoville Heat Units.

Scientifically, breakfast is not the most important meal of the day. This was a catch phrase that was developed by an advertiser in 1944 to market General Foods cereals.

The "Sell Buy" date placed on egg cartons does not indicate the date when eggs "go bad" (and are unfit for consumption). This date is a suggested date for the seller based on the estimate for when the eggs will stay their freshest. Next to this date, is a three-digit number that indicates when the eggs were cleaned and packaged. The number is the calendar date starting with January 1st (001) through December 31st (365). If you want to know how fresh an egg is, drop it (gently) into a glass of room temperature water. If the egg floats, throw it out (in the garbage, not at a Bears fan). If the egg sinks to the bottom, it is still good. The faster it sinks, the fresher it is.

To expose the poor working conditions in American factories at the turn of the 19th Century, the writer Upton Sinclair went undercover in a meatpacking plant in Chicago. After observing the poor working conditions, including child labor, he published his book, 'The Jungle', in 1906. Instead of bringing attention to the plight of lower-class workers, the public's reaction to 'The Jungle' focused on the descriptions of the unsanitary conditions in which the meat was butchered and processed. Americans were so disgusted and outraged that President Theodore Roosevelt took action to investigate the factories and then pass legislation to regulate the meat-packing industry. This eventually led to the creation of the Food and Drug Administration (FDA).

Ever heard of "Anchor Pricing"? Grocery stores and restaurants have. When it comes to human psychology, we can't categorize items as cheap or expensive without a comparison. Prices are relative. In a grocery store, the anchor price is when the original price is displayed along with the sale price so that consumers can see how much they are saving. This ratio drives your desire to buy the product without considering whether or not the sale price is a good value on its own. For restaurants, have you ever noticed that there is always one very expensive entrée or over-priced bottle of wine? I'm not interested in spending $40 on a steak. But if there are similar steaks on the menu that are $60 dollars, the $40 ribeye doesn't sound that expensive in comparison. Same with wine. If there are only two options for wine, most people will select the least expensive one. $20 dollars is more appealing than the $40 dollar variety. Now add the science of "anchor pricing" and list one or two bottles for $75. With three options, the probability increases that people choose the middle option, focusing on the fact that they are saving $35 dollars in place of spending an extra $20 dollars. Planning for, and playing on, this probability increases profits.

WINGS

There is nothing in this world better than a chicken wing. Baked, grilled, fried, smoked. Brined, dry rubbed, sauced. Sweet, hot, salty, crispy. The possibilities are endless – as is my love for them.

I don't remember the first time I ever had "Buffalo Wings" but it must have been love at first taste. This was a time before social media, reality TV shows, and the popularity of quinoa – you know, the good ole' days. These were the days before almost every restaurant had Wings on their menu, as at that time, they were considered "bar fare". And rightly so. What pairs better than spicy fried chicken and an ice-cold pint? To make Wings at home involved asking the butcher to save the wings for you as they were usually discarded when the bird was broken down. Nowadays, Wings are everywhere. You can even find them under a heat-lamp at some gas stations. And to buy a pound of them at the store now is sometimes as expensive as buying a steak. Society. How far we've come.

If you know me, then you know that the following sentence is not hyperbole. I eat wings once or twice a week. During the Atkins craze you would have thought I'd actually lose weight (I blame the ice-cold pints, not my precious wings). Why not have them every week (or more)? There are so many different variations that you could circle through the culinary styles of the world just with chicken wings. And if you needed any other reason to sell you on this 8th Wonder of the World, chicken wings are packed with collagen. So the more you eat, the more health benefits you'll reap. Better digestion, reduces inflammation, improves your immune system, helps with joint pain and arthritis, and forms elastin – which fills in wrinkles. Think of the money you'll save on spa treatments and Botox.

WHOLE OR SEGMENTED

The first consideration is whether or not you want the wings whole or segmented. Each wing is made up of three segments: the drumette, the flat, and the tip. When chicken wings are not served whole, they are usually served as a combination of drumettes and flats, with the small, thin tips discarded. There are pros and cons to each style as well as personal preference. My preference is based on how the wings will be prepared.

Smoked Wings:	Whole
Grilled/BBQ Wings:	Whole
Deep Fried:	Segments
Oven Baked:	Either
Microwaved:	Just kidding

PREFERRED COOKING METHOD

Deep frying is traditional and yields the crispiest wing. Unless you have a restaurant-grade commercial fryer in your home, pot frying or using small countertop fryers don't deliver the same ease of cooking or consistent product. I'm also not a fan of the post-fry grease-stank that fills your house afterwards (and seems to linger for hours).

Grilling is nice if you have the ability to rock a wood or charcoal fire, or kick on a propane grill, whenever you want. I like the flame-kissed texture and flavor of grilling but this requires some trial and error and it's best if you don't wander off as the difference between crispy chicken skin and blackened ash can be a few short seconds of inattention.

This brings us to the oven. Most people have one. The temperature is easy to control and the heat remains constant. You also don't have to stare through the oven window worrying about flare-ups. Setting a timer and walking away is certainly the easiest way to make dinner. The downside is that you sacrifice that desired crispiness. But there is a way to find the sweet spot between all of the different cooking mediums to ensure that the wings are juicy and tender but still have that delicious crispy skin: The 2-Temp Technique (T3). Once you master the basic **T3 Wing Recipe** then it's time to flip through the following pages and explore the different sauces and flavor options.

T3: 2-TEMP TECHNIQUE CHICKEN WINGS

Starting the wings off in the oven on a very low temperature pulls some of the fat out of the skin (so that they can crisp up) and then bastes the wing in the rendered fat (so the meat stays tender and doesn't dry out). Finishing the wings at a very high temperature further crisps the skin. You can use the following culinary cheat codes to further improve your oven baked wings: flour, or better yet, rice flour, and baking powder.

A dry wing is a crispy wing. To prepare your wings (whether whole or segmented), pat, roll, press, and/or squeeze each wing with a towel or paper-towel to remove as much excess liquid as you can. Pat, pat, pat. Dry, dry, dry. You want them as dry as you can possibly make them. If possible, do this a day ahead of time and then let them further dry out in the fridge overnight. And then, just before cooking them, give them another round of paper-towel hugs.

Determine your serving size. My wife and I routinely knock back 8 wings (16 segments) between us (60/40 distribution 'cause I'm greedy and eat like the smallest jackal at the Kalahari buffet). So for us, our serving size is 3-4 whole wings / 6-8 wing segments (per person). If the wings aren't going to be the star of your supper show, you can dial this up or down depending on what else you're serving.

1 Preheat the oven to 270 degrees.

2 In a large bowl, mix the flour, baking powder, and salt.

3 Drop the wings in the flour mixture and give them a light dusting. They don't have to be coated. Shake off any excess.

4 Cover a baking pan or cooking sheet with aluminum foil (to catch the drippings) and place a wire rack on top. Place the wings, skin side up, on the wire rack so that they don't sit in the grease while they cook. Bake for 30 minutes.

5 Turn the heat up to 450 degrees and cook until they reach your desired level of crispiness (and an internal temperature of at least 160 degrees). About 20 mins.

Items You Should Always Have On Hand:
chicken wings

per 6-8 wings or 12-16 segments:
1/2 cup flour (or rice flour)
1 Tbs baking powder
1/2 tsp table salt

BISON WINGS

The word "buffalo" has come to represent more than just the large mammals which once roamed North America at will or for the second largest city in our 11th State. It's now synonymous with a condiment. "Buffalo Sauce" is traditionally made with bottled cayenne-pepper sauce and butter. As its history and initial use has been traced to fried chicken wings in Buffalo New York, the name stuck. Anything tossed in this sauce is now referred to as Buffalo Style. Over the past few years, thanks to the inter-web and social media, the increasing trend with wings and Buffalo Style sauces, is to see who can make the hottest one (and then challenge others to eat it). While I love the endorphin-releasing result of ingesting ass-burning food, I also like my food to taste good. Hard to enjoy the intricate flavor profiles of a Carolina Reaper when you're funnel-chugging milk and crying into your napkin (which is hopefully clean – don't make that eye-blinding mistake). This version of Buffalo-Style Wings has all the flavor of cayenne-pepper sauce but is milder and creamier than most traditional wing sauces.

Purists will tell you that you can only use Frank's RedHot Original Cayenne Pepper Sauce. Don't get me wrong, this is an awesome sauce. Not too spicy and really versatile. But the fun of cooking, and developing your own recipes, is personalizing them. So after making these wings with Frank's, try them with your other favorite hot sauces.

• enough for 6-8 wings •
(12-16 segments)

Scoville Scale:
1/4 cup hot sauce
1 ½ Tbs sour cream
2 Tbs unsalted butter (cold)

1 Get your wings cooking with the **T3 Wing Recipe** (pg. 35).

2 Over Low Heat, warm the hot sauce in a saucepan until it just starts to bubble.

3 Add the sour cream and stir until it dissolves into the warm hot sauce.

4 Turn off the heat. Stir in 1 Tbs of cold butter. Stir continually until the butter melts. Add the 2nd Tbs of cold butter and stir continually until it is melted completely into the sauce.

5 As soon as your wings are cooked, and still warm, toss them in the sauce and serve.

PELICAN WINGS

Every day can be Fat Tuesday with these wings. In place of a traditional, buffalo-style, sauced wing, these are tossed in a Cajun-style rub. The word "Cajun" often scares people away with the misplaced fear that they are spicy. While anything with cayenne pepper is going to have some heat, these wings are more savory-sweet than knock-you-on-your-ass hot. Without opening myself up to litigation, I'll just say that these wings are *digit-licking great!* Recommend pairing them with an ice-cold Abita or a Mint Julip. Laissez le bons temps roller.

1   Combine all the dry ingredients to make the
    Cajun Wing Rub.

2   In a saucepan, heat the vegetable oil over Low Heat. Melt
    the butter in the oil and stir together.

3   Add 1 to 1-1/2 Tbs dry rub (per 6 wings/12 segments).
    Simmer over Low Heat for 3-4 mins, stirring until the spices
    have time to party with the melted butter.

4   When the wings are cooked (**T3 Wing Recipe**, pg. 35) and
    ready for some Louisiana love, throw them into the pan
    and stir them through the sauce until they are coated.
    Plate. Pour any remaining sauce over the top. Serve with
    carrot and celery sticks, or just with more wings.

• 1/4 cup dry rub •
enough for about 18 wings
(36 segments)

Parish Party:
Cajun Wing Rub
   2 Tbs chili powder
   1 Tbs garlic powder
   1 Tbs onion powder
   1 Tbs dried oregano
   1/2 Tbs cayenne pepper
   1/2 Tbs lemon pepper
   1/4 Tbs table salt
1 Tbs vegetable oil
2 Tbs unsalted butter

37

CHINESE SALT & PEPPER WINGS

The Salt & Pepper in this recipe does not refer to the two most common spices in every person's kitchen. Nor does it refer to a hip-hop group from Queens. It's based on a popular Chinese style of dishes. These wings are a nice change-up from traditional Buffalo-Style. They can be made mild or they can be made hot if you want to push it. Push it good. P-push it real good.

• enough for 6-8 wings •
(12-16 segments)

Set List
1/4 cup chopped jalapenos
  (1-2 peppers)
2 Tbs chopped garlic (4 cloves)
1/4 cup chopped green onions
2 Tbs vegetable oil
1/2 tsp coarse ground salt

1 Start cooking your wings with the **T3 Wing Recipe** (pg. 35).

2 Slice the top off each pepper to remove the stem. Cut in half lengthwise and lay the jalapenos flat, seed-side up, on a cutting board. Lay your knife on its side and slice down the length of the pepper to remove the seeds and the lighter colored veins. (This is where the heat lives so if you like a little fire with your wings, leave the veins, and/or seeds, in.) Cut the jalapenos into strips and then chop into chunks.

3 Peel the garlic and slice the tip off each clove. Rough chop into thick chunks.

4 Slice the end off of each green onion. Cut into wide slices (green part and the white part).

5 Add the vegetable oil to a pan heated over Medium Heat.

6 Sauté the jalapenos and garlic for 4-5 minutes. Turn the heat off and then add the green onions and the salt. Stir together.

7 Add the cooked wings to the pan and work them through the sauce to absorb the flavor. Plate and then spoon the rest of the sauce over the top.

BALROG FIRE WINGS

You shall not pass (up an opportunity to try these fiery sweet wings). Forged in the Mines of Moria, the blazing heat of the habaneros is tempered with the sweetness of the mangos. This fellowship makes for a tasty wing that can be tamed by seeding and de-veining the peppers should you desire less of a battle. But if you're a pepper aficionado, then you know that the magic of a good pepper is all of those endorphins that get released in your brain. So if you dare, then take the journey to the Misty Mountains and try crossing the Bridge of Khazad-dûm to brave these Fire Wings – the one wing to rule them all.

• 12 oz of sauce •
4 oz of sauce is good for 6 wings
(12 wing segments)

Tolkien's Tome:
2-6 finely diced habanero peppers
    2 peppers for Mild
    4 peppers for Hot
    6 peppers if you are Sauron
1 mango
1 cup sugar
1/2 cup water
1/2 cup white vinegar
1/2 Tbs table salt

1 Prep the wings and get them in the oven (according to the **T3 Wing Recipe**, pg. 35).

2 While the wings are getting crispy, remove the stems from the habanero peppers. For a milder wing sauce, remove and discard the seeds and the veins. Finely dice and add them to a saucepan.

3 Slice the mango away from the pit and scrape the meat from the skin. Chop into small chunks and add the fruit into the pan.

4 Over Medium Heat, cook the mango and the habaneros for 4-5 minutes to soften them up and give them some exposure to the hot pan – this will help bring the sugars out and add some sweetness to the sauce. Stir occasionally but be careful about leaning over the pan unless you are congested and want to turn your nose into a faucet.

-37.858419, 175.680653

5 Add the rest of the ingredients and stir until the sugar dissolves. Using a hand mixer or a blender, bring the ingredients together and mix/blend until the consistency is smooth and not chunky.

(If you're using a blender, let the sauce cool before trying to blend. If you're as impatient as I am, or you relish the challenge of blending hot liquids, make sure the lid is firmly attached – AND push down on the lid with one hand – AND work the blender through its LOWEST setting.
Hot liquid + blender + loose lid or highest setting = the fires of Mordor erupting into your face and spraying lava all over your ceiling.)

6 If you used a blender in place of a hand mixer, add the sauce back to the pan. Simmer over Low Heat for 8-10 mins until the sauce thickens to your liking.

7 When the wings are done cooking, and nice and crispy, toss the wings in the sauce and serve for Breakfast, Second Breakfast, Elevensies, Luncheon, Afternoon Tea, Dinner, or Supper.

 Make the hot sauce on your grill – outside. This will not only keep your wallpaper from peeling but is also pretty effective at keeping the mosquitos away.

Mango-Habanero Shrimp Skewers are grilled in the same sauce. If you have any sauce leftover, get working on some shrimp skewers.

NASHVILLE SCORNED CHICKEN

This sauce is rumored to have been created almost a hundred years ago by a jilted woman to punish her boyfriend's "wandering affections". When he returned home at sunup, after a night out on the town, she scavenged her cupboards for every spice and pepper available and whipped up the hottest sauce she could concoct. She then poured it all over his favorite meal, fried chicken. The hot sauce wound up being more pleasurable than painful, and as a result, this regional style of spicy fried chicken has spread beyond Nashville and around the world. While this pioneer of wing sauce moved on with her life and has since been lost to history, her legacy remains in what we now refer to as Nashville Hot Chicken.

• enough for up to 8 wings •
(16 wing segments)

Prince's Provisions:
1/2 cup vegetable oil
1 Tbs brown sugar
1 tsp honey
1 tsp black pepper
1 tsp smoked paprika
1 tsp garlic powder
1 tsp table salt
cayenne pepper

1 Determine your bravery level based on the Cayenne Heat Level Index below.

2 Whisk all ingredients together.

3 When the wings are done cooking (**T3 Wing Recipe**, pg. 35), and still warm, drizzle this thick sauce over them and serve.

Heat Levels:
Flamethrower = 1 tsp cayenne pepper
Trinitrotoluene = 2 tsp cayenne pepper
Composition C = 4 tsp cayenne pepper
Thermite Grenade = 2 Tbs cayenne pepper
The opening scene of 'Apocalypse Now' = 3 Tbs cayenne pepper

CODE-7 SMOKED WINGS

Where there's smoke, there's fire. But flames aren't the only way to BBQ. If you have a smoker, low and slow smoking is another option for expanding your wing repertoire. Takes some time and effort, but well worth the smokey BBQ finish that can't be reproduced on a grill or in the oven. So get your smoke-box blazing and take a break from traditional wings.

• enough for 8 wings •
(16 segments)

CAD Status:
4 cups water
1 cup apple juice
1/2 cup kosher salt
2 Tbs brown sugar
1 Tbs chili powder
1 Tbs minced garlic
1 Tbs onion powder

1 Combine the water and the apple juice in a pot. Stir in the dry ingredients and warm over Medium Heat. Stir occasionally until the salt and sugar dissolve.

2 Let the brine cool to room temperature before adding the wings. This can take an hour or two so be patient. Once it's cooled, submerge the wings in the brine and let them sit in the fridge for 4-12 hours.

3 When you're ready to deploy, remove the wings from the brine, give them a good rinse in cold water, and then pat them dry. Place the wings on the smoker and smoke at 250 degrees for 1 ½ - 2 hours (internal temp should be 160 degrees).

(K+) If you don't want to wait for the brine to cool use this trick: Only use 1 cup of water to dissolve the solids and spices. Then add ice to the brine. This will both cool the brine, and then as the ice melts, provide the rest of the water. But 1 cup of ice does not equal 1 cup of water. Depending on what shape and size your ice is, you'll notice that a filled cup will have gaps in it. Just experiment with your ice ahead of time to determine how much is needed to melt into the appropriate amount of water.

ALABAMA BBQ SAUCE

This white BBQ sauce provides a good balance to the smokiness of BBQ or wood-fired meat. Drizzle it over chicken wings, BBQ pork, smoked ribs, or even cardboard – it's that delicious. Make up a double batch so that you can bathe in it. If you're making **Code-7 Smoked Wings**, you'd be remiss if you didn't make this Alabama style white BBQ Sauce as well.

Roll Tide:
1/2 cup mayo
2 ½ Tbs apple cider vinegar
1 tsp mustard
   (brown or creole)
1 tsp Worcestershire Sauce
1/4 tsp coarse ground salt
1/4 tsp garlic powder
1/4 tsp black pepper
1/4 tsp onion powder

1 Whisk all of the ingredients together. Let the sauce sit in the fridge for at least an hour to really bring the flavors together.

 The buttery richness of garlic bread rounds out the vinegary tartness of **Alabama BBQ Sauce**.

 If you want to level up your garlic bread game, make them with King's Original Hawaiian Rolls.

WING DIPPERS

What do you dip your Wings in? (If the answer is ketchup, then it is imperative that you read the chapter: **The World's Worst Food**.) Other than restaurants trying to be avant-garde and offering smoke-infused mango chutney with pomegranate seeds and a zest of kumquat, the traditional two choices of dipping sauce are **Blue Cheese Dressing** or **Ranch Dip**. Your preference in this area defines you as a human-being as personalities are polarized to one or the other. Consider what Mia Wallace tells Vincent Vega:

> *"My theory is that when it comes to important subjects, there's only two ways a person can answer. For instance, there's two kinds of people in this world, Elvis people and Beatles people. Now Beatles people can like Elvis. And Elvis people can like the Beatles. But nobody likes them both equally. Somewhere you have to make a choice. And that choice tells me who you are."*

Can you buy these sauces premade? Of course. But where's the fun in that? Pick your favorite sauce and give one of these recipes a try. But choose wisely. As your choice tells me who you are…

BLUE CHEESE DRESSING

⚠️ For a really special dressing, try smoked Blue Cheese.

Chunky and Funky:
1 cup mayo
1 cup sour cream
1/2 cup buttermilk
2 Tbs apple cider vinegar
1 Tbs sugar
1 tsp Worcestershire Sauce
1/2 tsp garlic powder
1/2 tsp onion powder
1/2 tsp table salt
6 oz of blue cheese, crumbled

1 Buy a good brick of blue cheese and crumble it in place of purchasing a pre-packaged crumbled cheese.

2 Whisk all the ingredients together except for the blue cheese.

3 Fold in the blue cheese so that the chunks remain intact. Place in the fridge to let the flavors set for at least 4 hours, overnight is best.

RANCH DIPPING SAUCE

Nectar of the Gods:
1/4 cup Italian parsley
2 Tbs chives
1 cup mayo
1/2 cup sour cream
1/2 cup buttermilk
1 tsp garlic powder
1/2 tsp coarse ground salt
1/2 tsp onion powder
1/2 tsp garlic powder
1/4 tsp dried dill

1 Remove the parsley leaves from the stems. Chop as finely as you can.

2 Finely dice the chives.

3 Combine the mayo, sour cream, and buttermilk. Add the rest of the ingredients and whisk everything together until it is smooth. Place in the fridge to let the flavors set for at least 4 hours, overnight is best.

PORK

In the late 1980s there was an advertising campaign to get more people to eat pork. It was marketed as "The Other White Meat". So sad that something so delicious was presented as the stepchild of the primary proteins. Pork dishes should be on your plate and not out in the middle of nowhere, a distant third to chicken and beef.

CREAM CITY BEER BRATS

Only noobs buy beer-flavored, or any other flavored, Bratwurst. Bratwurst should be ground pork, seasoned up to taste like a German bier haus, stuffed in a casing, and sold to you by your favorite fleisher. Some cookbooks avoid naming a specific brand, and I will adhere to that convention here, but if your preferred bratwurst is from Sheboygan Falls Wisconsin, then this isn't your first rodeo and you've already achieved master sausage status. To further pander to the State of my birth, my beer of choice is a lager born on December 30th, 1903. A 32-ounce bottle of crescent-moon-girl is enough for a 5-pack of brats.

Stuff you need to have or buy:
1 pack of bratwurst (5 brats)
1/2 yellow onion
32 oz of lager beer
1 pack soft rolls or French rolls
  (not hotdog buns)

1 Cut an onion in half. Slice each end off and then remove the top layer and discard. Slice the onion into thick strips and add to a large pot. Pour in the beer and add the brats.

2 Simmer over Low Heat for 30 mins. If the beer starts to boil, turn down the heat so that the liquid just slightly rolls and bubbles.

(Tips) If you have a pot that does not have plastic handles you can boil the brats on your grill outside in place of in your kitchen to avoid fumigating your home with the sweet smell of boiling beer (unless, like me, that is one of your favorite scents).

3 Remove the brats from the beer and grill them over Medium flames. After about two minutes, when grill marks appear, flip the brats to work up the other side. Cook to your preferred shade of deliciousness. Remove from the grill, snuggle them into a warm roll, and serve with your favorite Dusseldorf Style mustard.

TIME FOR THE CONDIMENT CONVERSATION

Would you use low-octane, cheap-ass gas to top off the tank of a 1961 Ferrari 250 GT California Spyder?

You wouldn't pour a warm can of generic diet cola into a tumbler of 18-year old, single malt, Speyside Scotch, would you?

Then don't, [using CAPS for effect], DON'T put ketchup on your brats! If this is your go-to condiment, then you better read the chapter on **The World's Worst Food.**

 Try your brats with the following:
Mustard (preferably not neon-bright yellow)
Sauerkraut
German Red Cabbage
Jalapeno Relish
Beer-Butter Onions

JALAPENO RELISH

Sometimes things aren't always what they appear to be. Your eyes can influence and fool you. Use the word "jalapeno" and those that don't like spicy food are going to act on their first impression and skip over the recipe and turn the page. But then you'd miss out on a kickass condiment that works great with burgers, brats, or dogs (both hotdogs and Shelties). The sweet brine of the pickle juice mellows out the jalapenos and onions into a well-rounded garnish that isn't too spicy. Promise. Don't be scared.

• enough for 6 brats or 4 burgers •

Double Dog Dare:
1/2 cup finely diced onion
1/2 cup pickle juice
1 tsp celery salt
1 cup diced kosher dill pickles
   (about 2-3 whole pickles)
1/4 cup diced pickled jalapenos

1 Dice the onions as finely as you can. Place in a bowl and add the pickle juice and celery salt. Starting with this step gives the pickle juice some time to mellow out the onions.

2 Slice the stems off the pickles. Make a thin slice lengthwise down the pickle to cut just enough off to make a flat side. This will help you cut the rest of the pickle without it rolling around. Slice into strips, then sticks, and then dice finely. Add to the bowl with the onions and pickle juice.

3 Finely dice the jalapenos and add to the mix. Stir all ingredients together and let sit in the fridge for at least an hour – but this relish will stay good in your fridge for a couple weeks.

(Tips) For the best quality, use whole pickles. If you take a shortcut and buy sliced pickles, you'll find that they don't retain their crunch as much as whole pickles that you've sliced yourself. Texture matters.

Leftover jalapenos or onions? Make some **Chinese Salt & Pepper Wings**.

BAVARIAN BEAVER BURGER

Why is this burger called a beaver? Because **dam** is it good! What if a burger and a bratwurst had a baby? Don't concern yourself with the anatomical questions, just dare to dream. Add a pretzel bun and some **Beer-Butter Onions** into the mix and you've got some quality Food Porn. Dam!

Dad Jokes:
1 pack of bratwurst (5)
1-2 Tbs unsalted butter
pretzel buns
mustard

1 Slice down the side of each brat and pull the casing off. Roll and press each one into a small burger patty. (They are already seasoned so you don't have to add anything to them.)

2 Heat a pan over Medium Heat. Add some butter to coat the bottom of the pan.

3 When the butter is melted, drop the burger patties in. Cook for 4-5 mins, flip, and then cook the 2nd side for 4-5 mins. Remove when the internal temp is 155 (will carry-over to 160).

4 Place on a pretzel bun and choose one or more of the following toppings:
    Beer-Butter Onions
    Mustard
    Jalapeno Relish
    Ketchup
    (if you don't know that I'm kidding, then you better check out the chapter on **The World's Worst Food**)

 Want to level up your credibility during the next Octoberfest? If you're going to put mustard on a brat or burger, try Alstertor brand Dusseldorf Style mustard. Köstlich!

 Serve with **German Red Cabbage** or **3-Beer German Potato Salad**

MR. DREK'S AKA PIZZA

AKA is the acronym for "Also Known As". Forget Austin Powers, the real International Man of Mystery is my brother. And when he's travelling the world on business, his alias is Mr. Drek. This recipe is several passport pages of delicious ingredients baked up into what's also known as Cajun Flatbread Pizza. The savory smooth flavor of the smoked Gouda cheese is a great travelling companion to the spicy Cajun Andouille Sausage. Your mission, should you choose to accept it, is to make a bunch of these pizzas for dinner. But if anyone asks where you got this recipe from... we never talked.

Passenger Manifest:
Naan Bread (or other flatbread)
1 Andouille Sausage
5-6 Tbs tomato paste
1/2 cup diced smoked gouda cheese
 (natural smoked, not "smoke flavored")
1 cup shredded mozzarella cheese
1/2 cup red onion, sliced
1/4 cup mushrooms, sliced

1 Cook or grill the Andouille Sausage (or buy pre-cooked). Slice into chunks with your Sykes-Fairbairn.

2 Spread the tomato paste onto the Naan Bread. Sprinkle on the diced smoked gouda, mozzarella, and sausage. Top with the onions and mushrooms.

3 Bake at 400 degrees to melt the cheese and crisp the Naan bread to your liking (about 6-8 minutes).

 Customization options are endless: pepperoni, lamb, ground beef, ground pork, sundried tomatoes, black olives, green olives, Kalamata olives, artichoke hearts, red peppers, caramelized yellow onions, fresh garlic, fresh basil, feta cheese, provolone cheese, cheddar cheese, olive oil, balsamic vinegar...

SOUTH STREET SEARED CHOPS

To call this a 'Southern' recipe would be a misnomer. This is a recipe from as far south as you can go without a passport. If you've been to the intersection of Whitehead and South Street, then you've also probably had some of the best Cuban food outside of Cuba. The key to these delicious chops is searing a good crust into them by pan-frying over high heat. And the garlic-cumin seasoning. And the limes. That's a lot of keys. But this is a lot of flavor.

Llaves:
2 porkchops
1 tsp coarse ground salt
1/2 tsp onion powder
1/2 tsp cumin
1/2 tsp garlic powder
1/2 tsp black pepper
vegetable oil
1 lime

1 Make the pork seasoning by mixing the salt, onion powder, cumin, garlic powder, and black pepper. Set aside about 1/2 tsp of this seasoning for later. With the rest of the seasoning, season both sides of the chops.

2 Heat a pan over High Heat. Give it some time to get really hot. Add enough oil to coat the bottom of the pan and then add the pork chops.

   For 1 ½-inch or larger ("king cut") chops, cook 3-4 mins without moving them around so that a nice crusty-sear can develop. Flip the chops and sear the second side for 3-4 mins. To finish them off, turn the heat down to Medium, flip the chops back to the first side, and cook until the internal temperature is 135 degrees (3-5 mins).

   For 3/4-inch chops, sear the first side for 3 mins, flip, and then sear the second side for 3-4 mins. Remove when the internal temperature is 135 degrees.

3 When done, remove from the pan and let them rest on a wire rack for 5 mins (temp will come up to 145 degrees). Squeeze the juice of 1/2 a lime over the top and then sprinkle them with the remaining seasoning that you set aside. Slice the remaining 1/2 lime into wedges as a garnish.

 Serve with **Cilantro-Lime Rice**.

24.5465266,-81.7974539

CILANTRO-LIME RICE

Rice is such a great food because it is versatile and takes on flavors really well. It is a canvas waiting to be Pollock'd. This dish is 1 brushstroke of garlic, 3 splatters of butter, and a collage of cilantro and green onions. The cilantro and lime are a perfect pairing for **South Street Seared Chops**, **Teri's Tacos**, or **Grilled Citrus-Shrimp Tacos**.

Art Supplies:
1 cup cooked rice
3 Tbs unsalted butter
1 tsp minced garlic
1/2 Tbs coarse ground salt
juice of 1 lime
1/2 cup chopped cilantro
1/4 cup diced green onion

1 Make 1 cup of rice on the stove top or in a rice steamer.

2 While the rice is steaming away, melt the butter in a small saucepan over Low Heat. Stir in the minced garlic and sauté for 3-4 mins.

3 Add the coarse ground salt and the juice of one lime. Give it a quick stir.

4 When the rice is done, spoon it into the saucepan and work it around so that it can absorb all the buttery goodness. Simmer for 4-5 mins, stirring occasionally. Turn off the heat and then fold the cilantro and green onions into the party.

This is a great way to make use of leftover rice. If you've got cooked rice hidden somewhere in the back of your fridge, let it come to room temperature and then add it to the sauce. The flavored butter will work its magic and bring the rice back to life.

CAJUN SMOTHERED CHOPS

There's a common saying in regards to smothering someone with love. If this applies to pork chops, then this is exactly how I would like to be smothered. These chops cook up in about 30 mins but will be gone in 3 bites. Don't eat the bone though - although I'd eat just about anything if this Cajun gravy was slathered on it.

Chop Shop:
3-4 pork chops
  (1/2 to 3/4-inch thick)
salt and pepper
1/2 cup + 3 Tbs flour
vegetable or olive oil
1/2 cup finely diced onion
1/2 cup finely diced celery
2 Tbs unsalted butter
1 tsp Cajun Seasoning
  (I prefer Tony Chachere's)
1/4 tsp cayenne pepper
  (optional)
1 Tbs minced garlic
2 cups chicken broth
1 Tbs Worcestershire Sauce

1 Heat a pan over Medium-High Heat.

2 While the pan is heating up, season the pork chops with salt and black pepper. While I love thick cut chops, this recipe works best with thinner chops. Dredge the chops in flour (1/2 cup of flour should be enough to coat 4 chops).

3 Add just enough oil to coat the bottom of the pan. Shake off any excess flour from the chops and then add them to the pan when the oil has heated up. Brown the chops on each side, 4-5 mins.

4 Finely dice the onion and celery.

5 Once the chops are browned, remove from the pan and set aside. Turn the heat down to Low.

6   Melt the butter in the pan. Add the onions, celery, and Cajun seasoning. For a sauce with a little more bite, add in some cayenne pepper. Sauté for 5-6 minutes until the celery and onions soften.

7   Add the minced garlic and cook for 2-3 mins.

8   Sprinkle in the remaining 3 Tbs of flour. Stir well (or whisk) to work the flour into the butter and veggies. Work out any clumps. Cook for 2-3 mins, stirring frequently.

9   Turn the heat up to Medium and add the chicken broth and Worcestershire Sauce. Heat, stirring frequently, until the sauce begins to bubble and thicken.

10   Turn the heat back to Low. Add the chops back into the sauce, cover the pan, and simmer for 6-8 minutes to finish them up. Serve with, or better yet – over, mashed potatoes or rice so that they can sop up the delicious Cajun gravy.

Make this into a meal worthy of the Vieux Carre. Add some **Grilled Carrots**, **Joey's Smokey-Sweet Grilled Corn**, or some **Double Baked Potatoes**.

THE HEARTBREAKER

• 3-4 sliders •

Cath Lab Equipment:
1 slab of pork belly
    1 – 1 ½ lbs
black pepper
salt
dinner rolls
unsalted butter

Why is this called the heartbreaker? Is it because pork is delicious? And bacon is delicious? And making a sandwich with thick-cut, salty pork goodness, slathered in butter, is so delicious that you'd be heartbroken not to shove one of these in your mouth and swallow it in one bite like a pelican knocking back a sardine? Maybe. Besides, calling these "STEMI Sliders" just doesn't have the same catchy ring to it. Unless you're a cardiologist.

1 Score the skin and fat by making slices 1/2 to 1 inch apart (but don't cut into the meat). This will take a very sharp knife as cutting through fat is like running across a pool filled with jello.

(Tips) Place the pork belly in the freezer for 30 mins. You don't want to freeze it solid, but if the fat layer is cold and semi-frozen, it is easier to score.

2 Sprinkle with black pepper and coat liberally with salt. Rub into the scored skin to get it down into the fat. Let it sit in the fridge, uncovered, overnight so that it can dry out and the salt has some time to work into the meat.

3 When you're ready to cook, remove the pork belly from the fridge and let it come up to room temperature while you pre-heat your oven to 325 degrees. Place the belly on a wire rack (to allow the fat to render out when cooking). Placing the wire rack on a cookie sheet covered in aluminum foil or parchment paper (to catch the drippings) will save you some greasy cleanup later.

4 Cook at 325 degrees for 2 hours. If the internal temp is 150, and the skin is crispy and golden brown, then you've successfully completed the procedure.

5 Remove from the oven and let sit for 20 mins. Peel off the crispy skin and set aside for delicious cracklin' snacks. Once cool enough to touch, cut the pork belly to fit whatever sized rolls you're going to use (3" x 3" if you're going to be badass and use King's brand Hawaiian Rolls.)

6 Place the rolls in the still warm oven for 2-3 mins to warm up. Remove, slice in half, and butter each side without shame. Snuggle the pork belly chunks into the warm, buttery bread, and enjoy the arrythmia.

⚠ Add **Pickled Onions**. The pickled vinegar-tartness balances the richness of the pork belly.

BURGERS

Immigrants sailing from the port of Hamburg brought a local steak recipe with them to New York. This ground 'Hamburg Steak' spread across the Empire State as each chef and restaurant added their own ingredients and embellished the dish to local tastes. At some point, in some city (the exact one is highly debated), the 'Hamburg Steak' was served between two slices of bread. Much like bourbon, the Blues, and blue jeans, 'Hamburgers' became an American invention and popular export around the globe. Unfortunately, burgers also became synonymous with another American cultural icon, Fast Food.

Fast Food chains have ruined what we consider a burger to be. Why settle for a paper-thin, frozen, reheated, overly salted patty of questionable meat, served upon soggy, steamed buns and slathered in ketchup? Burgers are a blank canvas that can, and should, be artistically created with different types of meat, cheese, toppings, condiments, and breads. They should be as varied as the different cultures and culinary preferences of those that immigrated to these United States. From lamb burgers with Feta cheese, to smoked pork burgers covered in crispy bacon, to grilled jalapeno-topped burgers with ghost-pepperjack queso, to flattop seared sliders served on tiny Hawaiian Rolls – burgers are affordable, easy to make, and the only limit is your creativity.

BASIC BURGER

The following is a simple way to season up ground beef, push them into patties, and cook them in a pan or over the flames of a grill. If you come home from your job as exhausted as I come home, planning and prepping a meal can be frustrating. This is why food delivery apps are so popular. But these burgers are so easy that you can season and pat them out on a Sunday afternoon, wrap them in parchment paper or plastic wrap, and then you've got Monday's dinner prepped and ready for a quick cook. (I like to make a bunch and cover Tuesday's dinner too.) The following burger recipes all start with this Basic Burger seasoning and cook times.

> **Patty Time**
> 1 lb ground beef (80/20 fat content)
> 1 ½ Tbs Worcestershire Sauce
> 1 ½ Tbs Hidden Valley Ranch Seasoning & Salad Dressing Mix
>   (or: 1 Tbs garlic powder and 2 tsp onion powder)
> 1/2 Tbs sugar
> 1 tsp table salt
> 1/2 tsp black pepper

1 Add the Worcestershire Sauce to the ground beef and work it through with the best tool in your kitchen – your hands.

2 Mix all of the dry spices together and then add to the ground beef. Mix well, but sparingly. Don't overwork the meat or it can get tough when cooked.

3 Separate the ground beef into the appropriate portions depending on how big you want your burgers.
>   Do you want sliders, quarter-pounders, or monster pub-style beasts?
>   What are you serving with the burgers?
>   How big are your buns?
>   And how big are the buns you bought for the burgers?

Have fun with fractions:

 A pound of ground beef split into four equal portions makes 1/4-lb burgers. This is a nice size if you're entertaining lots of people. The fun of holidays, parties, and BBQs, is the socialization. A smaller burger means you'll have more time, and more of your appetite, to enjoy appetizers, side dishes, and beverages.

 For 1/3-lb burgers, divide the ground beef into three equal portions. This is a nice size for a regular lunch or dinner. These are perfect for my wife and I as we each get one burger for dinner, and then I've got one leftover for my lunch the following day.

 If you're ready for an exclusive relationship with a burger, split the ground beef in half and pat out some 1/2 pounders (like the **Deadwood Burger**)

4 Roll each portion into a ball and then flatten into 1/2-inch to 3/4-inch patties (depending on the size of the buns you're going to use).

5 However you cook your burgers, give them time to come to room temperature before dropping them on the heat. This will help with an even and thorough cook.

COOK 'EM UP

The times below are approximate and based on an 8 to 10 degree carryover cook. Meaning: once the burger is removed from the pan or grill, the meat will continue to cook for 3-4 mins raising the internal temperature another 8 to 10 degrees.

Legalese: While the ground beef you buy at your local market has been processed and ground in accordance with USDA standards, it is still recommended that hamburger be cooked Well Done (to an internal temperature of 160 degrees). Depending on what kind of burger I'm in the mood for, sometimes I like the texture of Medium or Medium Well. As long as your food storage and handling practices are on point, you shouldn't need to settle for Well Done for all your burgers. But they (you know, *THEY*) say 160 degrees is the safe zone.

Flattop Burgers:
Heat a pan over Medium-High Heat. Add 1 Tbs vegetable or olive oil and 1 Tbs butter. When the butter melts, lay the patties in the pan.

> For Medium: Cook for 3 mins. Flip. Cook for 2 ½ mins.
> (remove from the pan when the internal temp is about 140 degrees)

> For Medium Well: Cook for 3 ½ mins. Flip. Cook for 3 mins.
> (remove when the internal temp is about 150 degrees)

> For Well Done: Cook for 4 mins. Flip. Cook for 3 ½ mins.
> (remove when the internal temp is about 155 degrees)

If you're adding cheese, add it when you have 2 mins of cook time left. If the cheese isn't melted to your liking after the cook time, add 1-2 Tbs of water to the pan, cover, and let the steam melt the cheese.

Grilled:
Over Medium-High Heat, grill with the lid open to monitor for flare-ups.

> Medium: Cook for 4 mins. Flip, Cook for 3 mins.
> (remove from the grill when the internal temp is about 140 degrees)

> Medium Well: Cook for 5 mins. Flip. Cook for 3 1/2 mins.
> (remove when the internal temp is about 150 degrees)

> Well Done: Cook for 5 mins. Flip. Cook for 4 1/2 mins.
> (remove when the internal temp is about 155 degrees)

For cheeseburgers, add the cheese when you have 3 mins of cook time left.

 With the back of a spoon (or your thumb), push down in the middle of the patty to make a small depression. This will help keep the burgers flat when they cook so they don't balloon up in the middle.

 Market Deli Seafood Salad, Rogue Squadron Salad Bites, Creamy Cool-Slaw, 3-Beer German Potato Salad, Hawaiian Mac Salad, Festival Fare Mozz Stick, and especially – **Aunt Jo's Holiday Shrimp Dip.**

BREWSKI BURGER

Brew. Brewage. A cold one. A tall boy. A road soda. Hop juice. Liquid bread. Laughing water. A barley sandwich. Suds. Ale. A pint. A tinnie. Cerveza. Cerveja. Bier. Bière. Birra. Or just, "beer". Is there a more perfect food than beer? Water, barley, hops, (and yeast). Hard to argue with a recipe that has been a standard since 1516. Burgers and beer go together like wine and cheese, or sushi and sake. Ya rarely see one without the other. In place of having your brew *with* your burger, why not have it *with, in*, and *on*, your burger?

Cullen-Harrison Act:
1 lb seasoned ground beef
2 oz beer (1/4 cup) + 2 Tbs
2 Tbs unsalted butter
1 Tbs flour
1/4 cup milk
1 cup shredded cheddar
   cheese
1-2 tsp coarse ground salt
cooked bacon
Beer-Butter Onions
pretzel bun

1 Replace the Worcestershire Sauce in the **Basic Burger** recipe (pg. 57) with 2 Tbs of your favorite beer and then cook up your patties. Set aside while you make the beer-cheese sauce.

2 In a saucepan, melt the butter over Low Heat. Add the flour and whisk continually for 2-3 mins to break up any lumps and brown the flour a bit.

3 Mix the milk and the 2 oz of beer. (The type of beer you add will impart a lot of flavor into the sauce – so use something you enjoy.) Pour into the pan and whisk continually to bring everything together. Let the sauce simmer until it just starts to bubble (4-5 mins) but do not let the sauce boil.

4 Turn the heat off. Add the cheese, a small handful (about 2 Tbs) at a time, and stir until it is completely melted. Repeat and continue until all the cheese is melted into the sauce. Stir in the salt (add more/less to taste). While tempting, try not to drink this directly from the pan. You'll want to save some to pour all over your burger. (I won't judge you for whatever happens to the leftovers.)

(Tips) Pre-shredded cheese can get a little grainy when it melts down into the sauce. For the creamiest sauce, buy your cheese whole (in a brick) and shred it yourself.

5 Build it: Bottom bun, burger, beer-cheese sauce, **Beer-Butter Onions**, bacon, more bacon, maybe more beer-cheese sauce, top bun. But what to do with the leftover beer?

XP: 30

BEER-BUTTER ONIONS

Delicious on burgers – especially the **Brewski Burger** – but also good on **Cream City Brats**. Spoon them onto the bun and let the bread sop up the buttery-beer goodness.

Bulb 'n Brew:
1/2 an onion (yellow or sweet)
4 Tbs unsalted butter
1/2 tsp coarse ground salt
1/4 tsp black pepper
1/4 cup (2 oz) of your favorite beer

1 Slice the onion as finely as your knife work allows. Long thin strips work best. (1/2 an onion is enough for 4 burgers or a 5-pack of brats.)

2 Melt the butter over Low Heat in a sauce pan. Add the salt and black pepper and simmer for 2 mins. Add the onions and stir to coat in the butter. Let them cook down for 3-4 mins.

3 Stir in the beer and simmer until the onions are super soft and turn from white to a beer-brown. (10 mins)

60

BOX ALARM BURGER

Grab your SCBA because this burger is a worker. Charring the jalapenos provides some nice color and texture but also allows you to control the level of spiciness. The less you leave it over the heat, the hotter it will be (if ya follow that logic). So like a BC, you get to call the shots. Attach pepper-jack cheese and some spicy mayo to build out the assignment.

Bunker Gear:
jalapeno peppers
1/4 tsp chili powder
1/4 tsp garlic powder
pinch of black pepper
2 Tbs mayo
1-2 tsp hot sauce
pepper-jack cheese
avocado slices

1 Slice the jalapeno(s) in half lengthwise. Over Medium-High Heat, grill each side for 3-4 mins until they start to blister and char. Alternatively, you can make these on your stovetop by laying them right on the burners for 4-5 mins a side over Medium-High.

2 Mix the dry spices with the mayo and then add in your favorite hot sauce to taste (1-2 tsp). Stir to bring the flavors together.

3 Season up your beef and sear or grill your burgers with the **Basic Burger** recipe (pg. 57).

4 Build it: bottom bun, spicy mayo, cooked burger, melted pepper-jack cheese, charred jalapeno slices, avocado, and then the top bun.

 What else would you want to pair this burger with but **Creamy Cool-Slaw** to douse the flavor-flames.

DEADWOOD BURGER

Pub style burgers, and tavern fare in general, must be cooked up quickly to satisfy the waiting patrons. The saloons of frontier mining towns couldn't afford to have their clientele take their business elsewhere – or get impatient and start shooting the place up. While this is a quick and simple burger to make, the 1/2-pound monster patty is no joke. So after a long day of working the ground for gold, or working the miners for their money, who wouldn't be ready for a shot of whiskey, a draft beer, and a giant burger? And if you're playing poker too, just make sure your seat is facing the door.

1876 Wagon Train:
1/2 lb burgers (1-inch thick)
1 Tbs vegetable or olive oil
1 Tbs butter

Pub Salt
2 parts table salt
2 parts sugar
1 ½ parts onion powder
1 ½ parts black pepper

Pick a bun
Choose a cheese
Select some veggies
Add some bacon?
Condiments?

1 Since these burgers are 1-inch thick, you'll have to cook them longer than the **Basic Burger** recipes. Heat a pan over Medium-High Heat. Add the oil, and once it's warm, melt the butter in it.

For Medium: Cook for 5 mins. Flip. Cook for 4 mins.
(remove from the pan when the internal temp is 130-135)

For Medium Well: Cook for 5 ½ mins. Flip. Cook for 5 mins.
(remove when the internal temp is 140-145 degrees)

For Well Done: Cook for 6 mins. Flip. Cook for 6 mins.
(remove when the internal temp is 150-155 degrees)

2 After cooking up the 1/2-pound burger, throw it on the bun and dust it with some **Pub Salt**.

3 Build it: Top with traditional burger veggies, your favorite cheese and the condiments of your choosing. If you really want to be a badass, serve it on a plate made of bacon. Then you don't have any dishes to wash. You can just eat them.

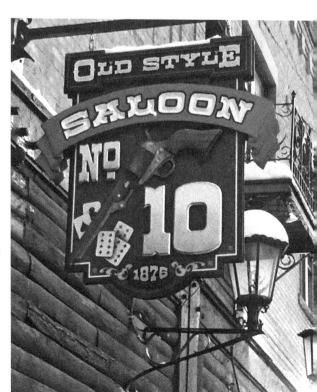

44.3771500, -103.729900

HAOLE SLIDERS

Who wouldn't want to live in Hawaii? Pristine beaches. Delicious food. Beautiful culture. All ruined by stupid tourists. Who probably all return home and say "we should move to Hawaii". How would you feel if you weren't able to take your kids to the neighborhood park in your suburb because it was constantly packed with people? Or you couldn't just drop in at the corner pub or restaurant because there was never any seating for you, a local, just trying to get a burger and a pint after a hard day's work? Or you couldn't even get home from work because pedestrians were wandering aimlessly in the streets taking photographs of the historic Walmart in your Edge City? Bummer, huh? So treat the Islands with respect. Remember that people live and work there and that our 50th State doesn't exist solely for your annual 2-week summer vaycay. Maybe sit this year out. Stay home and make these sliders instead.

Staycation Itinerary:
1 lb seasoned ground beef
Canadian Bacon (or ham)
King's Hawaiian, Original
    Sweet Rolls
American cheese

1 Season the ground beef with the **Basic Burger** recipe (pg. 57).

2 Press the ground beef out on a sheet of parchment paper (or large cutting board) to a depth of 1/2-inch. Using a round cookie cutter, or a small glass, push out the burgers into a size that is slightly larger than the bread you are going to use.
For King's Hawaiian Rolls (slider size), the burgers should have a 3-inch diameter.

3 With the back of a spoon (or your thumb), push down in the middle of the patty to make a small depression. This will help the burgers retain their slider size and not cook up into pear-shaped meat-globes.

4 Cook the burgers in a pan or on the grill to your desired doneness.

5 While they are cooking, brown the Canadian Bacon (3-4 mins a side in the pan or on the grill).

6 Build it: slice the slider buns in half and place the cooked burgers on the bottom bun, layer with a small piece of American cheese, and top with some browned Canadian Bacon.

 Make this an Island pairing and serve with the **Hawaiian Mac Salad**.

FUN FOODS

Do you like cheese? Who doesn't, right? Ever had Casu Marzu? It's a pecorino from Sardinia that is left out for the flies to lay their eggs in. When the larvae hatch, they eat through the cheese digesting it, and softening it, as they go. This creamy delicacy is then enjoyed – maggots and all.

Hákarl is the national dish of Iceland. It's shark. Shark left out in the sun. Shark left out in the sun for several months. Shark left out in the sun for several months until it rots and begins to decay. If you can get past the overwhelming smell of ammonia, some say this dish is delicious. Some say.

Beer is made from yeast. After it eats up all the sugars to make alcohol, it settles in the bottom of the vat where most breweries just throw it out. But the enterprising Brits and Aussies scooped up this salty brown paste and spread it on their toast. If you've ever had Marmite or Vegemite, then you've eaten this yeast extract.

North of Phnom Penh Cambodia is a village called Skuon Spider Town. Guess what it's famous for? Seasoned and fried tarantula. When I heard that these giant spiders tasted like crab, I was in – even though I'm a card carrying arachnophobe. While it wasn't the cheapest item to mail order, it was more affordable than a trip to Cambodia. Don't know that it tasted like crab, but it wasn't horrible either. Cross that one off my Bucket List.

I love Blue Cheese but I don't think that I'd pay almost $400 a pound for it. Instead of cow's milk or sheep's milk, this variety of Blue Cheese is made with Moose Milk. And all from a single farm in Bjurholm, Sweden.

The Guolizhuang Restaurant in Beijing specializes in serving animal genitalia. Their menu includes over 30 types of different animal penises – roasted, fried, skewered, raw, and even a fondue dish. Deer, sheep, snake, seal, and a rather large offering named "Dragon in the Flame of Desire" which is a yak's most private part.

Need something delicious to wash all these unique foods down with? How about a cup of Black Ivory Coffee? They're Arabica Beans that are "processed" by Elephants. After they eat and digest them, they are removed from the elephants' droppings and made into coffee. The digestion process helps break down the beans and removes the bitterness that often accompanies coffee. Supposed to be a pretty smooth brew.

Tetrodotoxin is a neurotoxin that interrupts the nerve signals that direct organs to function. It is 1,000 times more toxic and deadly than cyanide. This toxin exists in a species of pufferfish that is a popular sashimi item in sushi restaurants. Preparation of Fugu is governed by law to ensure that the fish is filleted correctly to remove the toxin. Chefs must train, pass several tests, and complete an apprenticeship before they are licensed to prepare this dish. There is no antidote or antitoxin to Fugu tetrodotoxin.

If you're wondering if lobster, or Wagyu Beef, or perhaps truffles are the most expensive food, you'd be wrong. Would you believe that three of the most expensive foods on the planet are a spice, a chicken, and a melon?

$ Saffron is known as Red Gold because ounce for ounce it is more expensive than gold. It can only be harvested a few short weeks of the year and must be picked by hand.

$ Ayam Cemani Chickens are from Indonesia and are jet-black in color. Because it is believed that they have magical healing properties these chickens are between 2 and 3 *thousand* dollars each.

$ Yubari King Melons are a Japanese variety of cantaloupe with a perfectly round shape, smooth rind, and exceptional sweetness. At a food auction in 2019, a pair of these melons sold for 5 million yen – which is almost 50,000 US Dollars. That's 25K per melon.

Lest we judge and not be judged, what must other cultures think of Spam? This gelatinous cooked pork crammed into a tin can gained popularity during WWII as an alternative to trying to ship fresh meat overseas. Due to its long shelf life, the stockpiles that were shipped to the various Pacific Islands where Americans were stationed remained long after the war. Hawaii in particular has been culturally tied to this food as more Americans per capita purchase and eat Spam in this State than any other.

STEAK 'N BEEF

Other than lobster, or caviar, is there a food considered more top-end and luxurious than steak? Is there anything else that needs to be written? We're talking about steak here. Steak.

STEAK

Steak is expensive. You will be tempted to buy a cheaper cut of beef because steak is expensive. When I was younger, and single, and unemployed, I must have bought every cheap cut of cow at whatever crap-market was closest to my frat-house. Because steak is expensive. But the adage of "you get what you pay for" is true. Saving a few bucks just to chomp on sinewy, chewy, gristle-leather-meat is not a good use of your hard-earned cash. You might as well just light a ten-dollar bill on fire, eat the ashes, and save the trouble of cooking up a cheap-ass steak at all.

There's nothing wrong with being frugal or buying generic but there are just some things in life where you should treat yo'self. Refer to the following list of things you shouldn't go cheap on:

$ Toilet Paper
$ Sushi
$ Single Malt Scotch
$ Ammo
$ Steak

An entire nerd-book could be written on the differences between grass-fed and grain-fed cows, wet-aged versus dry-aged beef, and the USDA grading nomenclature; but for this humble book, and based on my humble wages, let's just focus on cuts of steak that are available at most local grocery stores. I prefer to apply this formula when selecting a steak.

Tenderness/Marbling + Thickness – Difficulty of Cooking = Ideal Steak

Tenderness
Have you ever been to a gym? I've heard of these places but am too busy drinking single-malt scotch, eating sushi, and wiping my ass with high-end, velvety-soft, super expensive toilet paper to lift any weights. But I'm sure you've been to, or at the very least heard of, a gym. Think of your average gym-rat rocking the free weights and building mass. Picture a sweaty, bulging, bicep. Is it rock hard? Would you want to chew on a steak that was rock hard? The best cuts of steak come from under-worked muscles because fat is flavor. Just like Gordon Gecko said in 1987: *"Fat is good. Fat is right. Fat works."* So the most tender cuts of beef come from the lazy, underworked, back of the cow.

Marbling
While tenderness is certainly preferred, it shouldn't be the only qualifying factor in selecting your cut of beef. I'll take flavor over tenderness every time. And flavor comes from the white fat-lines crisscrossing the steak like a highway map. This marbling helps the steak stay moist and juicy when cooking.

Thickness
The thicker the steak, the more meat you're paying for – but a thick cut is more forgiving if you happen to over-cook it. A thin steak can quickly go from a beautiful medium-rare to an aching Pterygoid muscle as you masticate the over-priced jerky.

Difficulty of Cooking

As the T-Bone and Porterhouse both contain a "T" shaped bone separating a long strip steak from a tenderloin steak, these cuts are the best of both worlds and are almost always what I order in a restaurant. But cooking one at home is difficult as each side of the bone requires a different heat and length of time to cook perfectly. I also steer clear of filet mignon. Unless you add some fat (like wrapping it in bacon), these steaks can over-cook quickly and don't have as much flavor as other less expensive cuts. I like a cut of meat that can be cooked in a pan as easily as it can on a grill. And yes, that pun three sentences back was intentional.

Based on these NASA-level calculations, the math reveals my three favorite cuts of steak to purchase and cook up at home: **#3** Porterhouse, **#2** New York Strip, and **#1**... Ribeye

THE DONENESS DEBATE

Should your steak be cooked to Well-Done, Medium, Medium Rare, or Rare?

If you've watched any cooking show on TV then you've no doubt seen that anyone who prefers a steak cooked to anything other than Medium Rare is taken out to the backyard and beaten upon the head-neck-chest area with a large wooden spoon. Probably dating myself here, but many of us were raised with the belief that cooked meat could contain no pink or ingestion would lead directly to intestinal fallout. My childhood understanding of steak was that you were supposed to chew each piece a dozen times to get it down. Don't buy into outdated mythology.

So how "done" should you cook your steak? As done as you like it. Critics be damned. If you like charred ash, then flame on, Johnny Storm. For me, the more steak I eat, the rarer I seem to like it. The first time I saw a rare steak I recoiled in horror at the pink, bloody terror. But then I tasted it. And sweet hallelujah was it delicious. So now I cook to Medium-Rare. (And don't worry, that "red" is only uncooked proteins – it's not blood.)

PREPARATION

According to television and the inter-web (which is never wrong), cooking a steak involves pan-searing it in a hot pan, basting it in herb-butter, and if it's a larger cut, finishing it off in the oven or under the broiler. I'm not opposed to all these steps, they do make a tasty steak, but my personal preference is grilling. If you're able to work up an actual wood fire, this is where it's at, as there's really no substitute for the smoke flavor and char brought on by a roaring fire. On those days when my job has sufficiently kicked my ass and reduced my energy and patience, and I just want to come home and have an easy dinner, then I'll pan-sear or compromise and use the propane grill. When I'm feeling lazy and unmotivated, propane is my best friend. (Teri is actually my best friend, but in this situation, a propane grill is a close second.) Either way, the keys to an amazing steak are:

- ⊙━ Preheating the grill or pan
- ⊙━ Making sure the steak is room temperature before cooking it
- ⊙━ Searing it over High Heat
- ⊙━ Undercooking it
  (so that the residual heat "carries the meat over" to the desired doneness)

And yes, size matters. The thicker your meat, the longer it needs to be over the heat. Reference the suggested cook times for both the pan-seared and grilled recipes. As always, you'll have to experiment with your own set-up and temperatures to find what works best for you.

PAN-SEARED STEAK

Searing a steak provides an awesome texture that you won't get on the grill. There's nothing like the contrast between the crust and the juicy meat as you slice into it and then savor the butter-basted goodness.

Arroser Agenda:
steak (1 - 1 ½ inch thick)
coarse ground Kosher salt
olive oil
2-3 peeled, smashed
   garlic cloves
5-6 sprigs of fresh thyme
   (or 1 tsp dried thyme)
1/2 Tbs fresh oregano
   (or 1/2 tsp dried)
1/2 tsp onion powder
1/2 tsp fresh Italian parsley
   (or 1/4 tsp dried)
4 Tbs unsalted butter

1 Season both sides of the steak liberally with coarse ground Kosher salt. Drizzle with olive oil. Set aside to come to room temperature.

2 Smash 2-3 garlic cloves and set aside. If using dried herbs, mix the spices together.

3 Get your pan hot over Medium-High Heat. (Cast Iron pans work great as they really retain and radiate the heat.) Drop in 2 Tbs of butter.

4 As soon as the butter melts, gently lay in your steak. Add the smashed garlic and the herbs (or dry spice mixture). Don't move the steak around in the pan – just let it develop a nice, seared crust.

For Medium Rare: sear for 4 mins.
For Medium: sear for 5 mins.
For Well Done: sear for 7 mins.

5 Add 2 more Tbs butter and then flip the steak. While it is cooking, spoon the herbed-butter over the top of the steak continually to baste it.

For Medium Rare: remove from the pan when the internal temp reaches 130 degrees
   (another 4-5 mins)
For Medium: remove when the internal temp reaches 140 degrees
   (another 5-6 mins)
For Well Done: remove when the internal temp hits 155 degrees
   (another 8-9 mins)

6 Remove from the pan and place on a wire rack to rest so that the carryover heat can work its magic.
4 minutes of rest for Medium Rare to 6 mins for Well Done.

THE SANDWICH OF BROTHERLY LOVE

The Sharks and the Jets. James Bond and Blofeld. Pat's King of Steaks and Geno's Steaks. Mortal enemies that have battled over the ages. While Passyunk Avenue is the Graceland of meat served on a long roll, there's no reason that tasty cheesesteaks can't be made in the comfort of your own home. You get extra points if the comfort of your home is actually in South Philly. Then you know how to make them wit' onions and "cheez".

Fud for Youse:
cooked steak
onions
sweet peppers
mushrooms
salt
black pepper
steak seasoning
rolls
cheese (try muenster
    or provolone)
mayo (optional)

1 Cut an onion into thin slices. Over Medium Heat, sauté the onion in some olive oil. About 5 mins.

2 Remove the stem and the seeds from the sweet peppers. Dice and then add to the pan with the onions. Cook down for 2-3 mins.

3 Add the sliced mushrooms and season with a pinch of salt and pepper. Cook with the onions and peppers for 3-4 mins and then remove all the veggies from the pan.

4 While long, thin slices of steak are traditional, it's difficult to cut thin enough without an industrial meat slicer. I prefer to just dice the steak into small chunks (the size of a sugar-cube). Season with your favorite steak seasoning.

5 Slice the rolls open and use as a reference to determine how much steak to use for each one. Add one portion of cooked steak into the pan and re-warm for 3-4 mins. Add the veggies and stir together.

6 Place 1-2 pieces of cheese (depending on the size of the roll) over the top and cover the pan so the heat melts the cheese.

7 Dress the roll with some mayo. With a spatula, slide the cheesy steak out of the pan and into the roll. Fly Eagles Fly!

 I love buying big steaks. Because the leftovers always get turned into one of these cheesesteaks.

GRILLED FLAT IRON STEAK

What's more tender than Filet Mignon but costs a lot less? Flat Iron Steaks are becoming more popular for both of these reasons and are popping up on most restaurants' menus. While they take marinades extremely well, I prefer a simple dry rub and some char-marks from a hot grill. While you can always cook a steak in a sizzling hot pan, under the broiler, or in the oven, my grandfather taught me right: a steak should be grilled. Spending summers with my grandparents in Door County taught me two things. First, that Wisconsin weather is unpredictable and can change quickly and often. And second, it didn't matter what the weather was like, my grandfather would pull out the small metal grill, pour in the charcoal, crumple up some old newspapers, and match light it up, rain or shine (or snow).

Bluff Buys:
Flat Iron Steak

#26 Seasoning
    2 tsp coarse ground Kosher salt
    1 tsp onion powder
    1/2 tsp black pepper
    1/2 tsp garlic powder
    1/2 tsp paprika
olive oil
Select your sauce

1 Sprinkle the **#26 Seasoning** liberally on both sides of the Flat Iron Steak. Rub into the meat. Drizzle with olive oil and place in the fridge to marinate for at least one hour (best if you can leave it overnight).

2 Select your sauce (**Chimichurri, Burgundy Mushroom Sauce, Green Onion Aioli**) and throw it together while the steak is marinating and your grill is coming up to temperature.

3 Remove the steak from the fridge at least 20 mins prior to grilling so that it has a chance to come up to room temperature.

4 Grill with the lid open (to monitor for flare-ups) for 5 minutes over the highest heat. Flip and cook the second side for 5 minutes. This will add some nice char-texture. To cook the steak the rest of the way through, move it off heat, so it is not over open flames, and close the lid. For Medium Rare, remove when the internal temp is 130 (about 8 mins). For Medium, remove when the internal temp is 135-140 (about 10 mins).

5 Once the steak is off the grill, let it sit for 4-5 mins before slicing so that it carryovers to the perfect doneness. Plate it, sauce it, and eat it.

45.244133, -87.113537

CHIMICHURRI

Parsley Party:
1/4 cup chopped Italian parsley
3 Tbs red wine vinegar
2 - 2½ Tbs fresh, chopped garlic
   (or 1 Tbs minced garlic)
1 Tbs dried oregano
1/2 Tbs coarse ground salt
1/8 tsp black pepper
1/2 cup extra virgin olive oil

 If you have leftover parsley (from another recipe or just as a garnish), whip up some of this sauce and then freeze it. It will last a few weeks in the freezer and thaws quickly when needed.

1 Add all of the ingredients, except the olive oil, to a blender. Give it a few pulses just to break up the parsley. Add the olive oil and give it 1-2 more pulses to bring it all together.

The sooner you can put this together, the longer the flavors have to work on their relationship and bond.

XP: 100

BURGUNDY MUSHROOM SAUCE

Grand Cru 'Shroom:
8 oz mushrooms
3 Tbs unsalted butter
1/2 Tbs coarse ground salt
1/8 tsp black pepper
1/2 cup Pinot Noir
   (use any red wine you enjoy)
1 ¼ cup of beef or chicken broth
1/2 tsp garlic powder
1 Tbs flour

1 Melt the butter in a pan over Medium Heat.

2 Add the mushrooms and season with the salt and pepper. Sauté for 3-4 mins.

3 Add the wine and cook for 2-3 minutes.

4 Pour in 1 cup of the broth and the garlic powder. Stir through the mushrooms and simmer for another 4-5 minutes.

5 Whisk the flour into the remaining 1/4 of broth until it is a smooth slurry (no lumps). Slowly pour into the mushroom sauce while stirring constantly. Once mixed together, simmer for 1-2 minutes until the sauce thickens. (If the sauce gets too thick, simply stir in a little more broth to thin it out.)

CAMPFIRE STEAK

Ya know that expression "it's the little things in life"? I find this to be true. The littlest things bring me the greatest joy. Here's a list of some of my favorite little things: Balvenie Portwood, a roaring wood fire, a Fuente Hemingway, and an oak-kissed slab of beef smothered in melted compound-butter. Who doesn't love campfires? And enjoying the outdoors? Whether camping, barbequing in your backyard, or just lighting up a propane grill on the balcony of your apartment, this is more than just a delicious meal – it's therapy. Year round, even in the snow, I'm huddled over the heat and losing my thoughts in the dancing red-orange flames wrapping around the logs while I swirl the lone ice-cube around my tumbler of Scotch with lazy snaps of my wrist. Throwing a steak over this crimson brilliance dissolves the stress of the day as my focus shifts to the anticipation of it searing and crisping to a beautiful shade of ebony-copper, melt-in-your-mouth, deliciousness. And life is good. Like the Stones say: *"You can't always get what you want. But if you try sometimes, you just might find, you get what you need."*

1 Season the steak with coarse ground Kosher salt and black pepper. Drizzle with olive oil. You can do this while the grill is heating up or ahead of time – even overnight. (If you're seasoning up your steak the day before, then go heavy with the salt. It will help pull some moisture from the meat, and then in turn, the meat will pull in the salt and help flavor the steak throughout.)

Poetic Prose:
steak (1 ½ - 2 inch thick)
coarse ground Kosher
salt black pepper
olive oil
1-2 Tbs unsalted butter

2 Get your grill going (wood, charcoal, or propane). Really work it up – you'll want it hot. I opt for a nice oak fire and use the smoke to provide an additional layer of flavor.

3 Lay the steak diagonally across the grates and sear for 2 mins over the hottest part of the grill. Do not cover or close the lid so that you can keep an eye on the steak to address any flare-ups.

4 Rotate the steak 90 degrees to set those super-badass "hashtag" grill marks you see in the movies. Sear for another 2 minutes.

5 Flip the steak to the opposite side and repeat the process. Sear for 2, rotate 90, sear for 2.

6 Move the steak off-heat so that it is not over open flames. Close the lid or cover the grill and cook to your desired doneness.

For Medium Rare, remove from the heat when the internal temp hits 125 degrees
(another 3-4 mins)
For Medium, remove from the heat as soon as the internal temp is 140 degrees
(another 5-6 mins)
For Well Done, remove from the heat at 155 degrees
(9-10 mins)

38.192813, -119.992929

7 After the steak is off the grill, let it rest for 4 minutes so that the carryover heat takes the internal temperature into the endzone and scores.

 Want to know the secret behind those amazing restaurant steaks? Salt and butter. KISS. Keep-It-Simple-Sunshine. The best steaks taste like... steak. So avoid marinades, flavor injectors, multiple dry spices, or sauces. When the steak is resting, just drop a Tbs of butter on top and sprinkle with a pinch of coarse ground salt. That's it.

BULGOGI SHORT RIBS

There are two types of short ribs. English Cut or Flanken Cut. An English Cut slices the ribs along and between the bones so that they stay intact between the chunks of meat. But a Flanken Cut slices across and through the bones so that each rib has a thin, round, slice of bone in it. Bones bring flavor. This cut, also called "Korean Style", is thin (1/4-inch to 1/2-inch thick) so they rock marinade really well and cook up quick.

There are also two types of people. Those that have enjoyed the smokey-sweet flavor of Bulgogi and those that will soon enjoy the smokey-sweet flavor of Bulgogi. So do yourself a favor and be a Bulgogi person. Be a Flanken Cut short rib person. Be a happy person and grill up these ribs.

Fire-Meat Marinade:
"Korean style" short ribs
    (3-4 per person)
1 Asian pear
    (or a red apple)
1 cup diced yellow onion
1/3 cup soy sauce
3 Tbs brown sugar
2 Tbs sesame oil
2 Tbs mirin (rice wine)
1 ½ Tbs minced garlic
1 Tbs honey
1/2 Tbs powdered ginger
1/2 tsp black pepper

1   Peel and core the pear. Dice as finely as your knife skills allow.

2   Peel and finely dice 1/2 a medium sized yellow onion (1 cup).

3   Place the diced pear and onion into a blender (or a large bowl if using a hand mixer). Add all of the other ingredients (except for the ribs, of course), and blend until the sauce is smooth.

4   Marinate the short ribs in the Bulgogi Sauce (in a large bowl or sealable plastic bag) in the fridge. 4 hours would be the minimum time to marinate but I prefer to leave overnight. Don't leave the ribs in the sauce for more than 24 hours though as it can start to break down the meat and the texture won't be as desirable after grilling.

5   When ready to grill these up, remove from the fridge and let the meat come to room temperature before throwing over the fire. Grill over Medium-Heat, with the lid open to monitor for sugar-induced flavor ups, for 5-6 mins a side.

TACOS

Have you heard of "Taco Tuesday?" How depressing. Why limit your intake of what is the World's greatest culinary invention to just 1/7th of your dinners? Why not have tacos every day of the week?

TERI'S TACOS

Have you ever played that game that involves the scenario: *"If you could only eat one food for the rest of your life, what would it be?"* My wife's answer is always "Tacos". Growing up and living most of her life in Central California, her knowledge of the taco-related culinary arts far exceeded my limited Mid-Western understanding of what a taco could be – which was the hard-shell, ground beef variety, smothered in jarred salsa from New York City. (Say it with me now: *"New York City?!!"*) This was probably the first recipe worked up for this book as we eat these tacos weekly. Uno mas, por favor.

Carne Asada:

1 ½ - 2 lbs Skirt Steak
   (or Flap Meat Steak)
1 cup orange juice
juice of 4 limes (about 1/2 cup)
1/4 cup diced cilantro
   (stems and leaves)
3 Tbs olive oil
2 Tbs cumin
1 Tbs minced garlic
1 Tbs coarse Kosher salt
1 Tbs chili powder
1 Tbs smoked paprika
1 Tbs Mexican oregano
1 Tbs onion powder

1 Combine all of the ingredients. Except the steak.
Using a blender or hand-mixer, blend into a marinade.

Note: If you're the type of person that would have blended the steak into a carne-colada had I not specifically added this exemption to the recipe, then you and your best friend Harry Dunne should drive the Shaggin' Wagon to Aspen – where the beer flows like wine and beautiful women instinctively flock like the salmon of Capistrano.

(Look it up if you're not following me on this one.)

2 Submerge the steak in the marinade (in a large bowl or a sealable plastic bag). Place in the fridge for at least 30 minutes but no more than 2 hours.

3 Remove the meat from the fridge and pour the marinade into a small pan. Set the steak aside to come up to room temperature as you fire up your grill (or heat a large pan (preferably cast-iron) over High Heat).

4 [Optional] Bring the marinade to a boil over Medium-Low Heat and continue to boil for 5 mins. Remove from the heat and set the sauce aside to use for basting or dipping.

5 Grill (or pan-sear) the steak over the highest heat possible for 2-3 mins per side. As this is a thin cut of steak, don't overcook it or it will be tough. Pink is your friend.

6 Let rest for 5 mins and then slice against the grain into strips or chunks (depending on your preference).

7 Warm your tortillas in a large pan over Medium-High Heat (2 mins a side) or directly on the grill or over a gas burner (1 min a side). Throw the meat into the warmed tortilla, add some or all of your favorite taco-fixings, and get crazy trying one or more of the following sides to Make-a-Meal.

Other Stuff You Need To Make Tacos:
Tortillas (flour or corn, any size you like)
Extra cilantro and limes
Cheese
Crema (sour cream)
Pickled jalapenos
Pickled Onions
Black olives

Guacamole
Mexican Cabbage Salsa
Curtido
Green Onion Aioli
Tomatillo Salsa
Fire charred Jalapenos
Refried Beans
Cilantro-Lime Rice

TACO TRUCK QUESADILLAS

Respect how awesome a food-vehicle the quesadilla is. Take a moment to ponder who the Rhodes Scholar was that first discovered the brilliance of melted cheese packed into a toasted flour tortilla. Consider the unlimited number of passengers that can be carried: different meats, vegetables, cheeses, and spices that can all be transported in a quesadilla from the pan to your waiting taste buds.

There are three secrets to making a stellar quesadilla:

SECRET #1:
A hot pan. You have to be patient. Wait for the pan to heat up before jumping offsides and losing 5 yards.

SECRET #2:
Butter (which is the secret to all delicious cooking). And real butter. This will brown the tortilla and help crisp it to the desired taco-truck quality you crave.

SECRET #3:
You want your quesadilla to be crispy not soggy.
If you take it from the hot pan, and drop it onto a flat surface (plate, cutting board, kitchen counter), the trapped heat will condense. Remember High School Science Class? Gas turns into Liquid. And a wet tortilla is a sad tortilla. So invest in a wire rack. Anything you want to be crispy or crunchy, cool it on a rack.

Truck Tires:
flour tortillas
unsalted butter
shredded Monterey jack cheese

For burrito sized tortillas (10-inch diameter):
2 cups of shredded Monterrey jack cheese

For taco sized tortillas (7-inch diameter):
1 cup of shredded Monterrey jack cheese

1 Heat a large pan over High Heat. Wait for it to heat up. Wait for it...

2 Drop a Tbs of butter into the pan and swirl it around as it melts to coat the entire bottom.
Place one tortilla into the pan and let it brown in the butter (2-3 mins).

3 If making a cheese-only quesadilla, sprinkle all the cheese into the center of the tortilla and spread it out towards the edges for maximum coverage. If adding meat or veggies, sprinkle on 1/2 of the cheese, add the meat/veggies, and then add the other 1/2 of the cheese to sandwich the goodies between the melty cheese layers.

4 Place another tortilla on top and push down into the cheese. Cook for 1-2 mins to melt the cheese.

5 Brush the top tortilla with melted butter and then flip to brown this side as well (2-3 mins).

6 When both sides are toasty brown and have some crispy crunch, remove from the pan and let rest on a wire rack for about a minute to cool slightly.

AZTEC AVOCADO SAUCE (GUACAMOLE)

When mom would come to visit, we'd stock up on avocados. Compared to the frozen tundra of the Badger State, alligator pears are almost always available in sunny California and it was a fun treat she couldn't get as readily, or as fresh, as she could at home. We'd mash up a bowl of guacamole with every meal – even breakfast – just to show mom we love her. The better the guacamole, the more frequently she'd visit. Wait... the reason for her visits were to spend time with me, right?

More than being authentic, smashing your guacamole is the best way to bring out the flavors. So if you have a mortar and pestle, mashing releases the oils and tasty bits. You can't really duplicate this by just stirring everything together. Besides, smashing your food is fun. Your mom would approve.

Molcajete Magic:
2 avocados
1 Tbs diced jalapeno (fresh, not pickled)
1/4 white onion, finely diced
1/8 cup cilantro, chopped
1/2 tsp coarse ground salt
1-2 Roma tomatoes, diced (1/2 cup)
juice of 1 lime

1 Remove the stem from the jalapeno and slice in half lengthwise (from the stem to the tip). For a milder guacamole, remove the seeds and the veins. For a guac with some bite, leave them in. Dice and then place in your smashing bowl.

2 Dice the onion and the cilantro and drop them into the bowl. Sprinkle in the salt. Now get to smashing. If you don't have a pestle, you can use any heavy, flat, object. Just push down firmly and twist to crush the peppers and onions and release their oils. Repeat until they are crushed (but you don't need to mash them into a paste).

3 Slice the avocados in half and remove the pits. Scoop the meat out into the bowl and stir it into the mashed jalapenos and onions.

4 Slice the stem-end off of the tomato and then slice in half lengthwise. Using a spoon, scrape out the seeds and discard. Chop the tomato into chunks and add them to the bowl. Squeeze in the lime and give it all a stir to finish up and get the fiesta going.

(Tips) Guacamole's arch nemesis is oxygen. If this battle existed in the Marvel Universe, there would be a trilogy and an origin-story movie detailing this epic saga. A prevailing myth is that if you save the avocado pit and place it in your completed guacamole, it will keep it from turning brown. But anyone that has tried this has no doubt been disappointed and left with gross, brown guac-a-muck.

The key is to remove the air. Grab a sheet of plastic wrap and push it down into the guacamole. Make sure that there is no space between the plastic wrap and the guacamole. Ensure maximum contact and then fix the edges of the plastic wrap around the bowl to complete the seal. This won't keep the guacamole fresh in your fridge for a week, but it will buy you at least an extra day or two.

GRILLED CITRUS-SHRIMP TACOS

Citrus-seasoned shrimp deserves to be grilled and wrapped in a warm tortilla the same way pigs should be baked into blankets and pizzas should be cooked into rolls. Quality cuisine, all three. This grilled shrimp is delicious on its own, but the fun of tacos is exploring the multiple combinations of salsas, sauces, and toppings. Try these with **Mexican Cabbage Salsa**, **Crema-Verde Dipping Sauce**, **Guacamole**, **Green Onion Aioli**, or if you're daring, **Ti-Malice Haitian Hot Sauce**.

• 4 tacos •

Tacklebox Gear
1 lb shrimp (13-15s)
3 limes
1 lemon
2 Tbs olive oil
1/4 cup chopped
   cilantro (stems okay)
1 Tbs minced garlic
1 tsp coarse ground salt
1/2 tsp chili powder
1/2 tsp black pepper
1/4 tsp onion powder
tortillas, small size
shredded cabbage

1 Squeeze the juice of 2 limes and the juice of 1 lemon into a bowl or blender. Add the olive oil, chopped cilantro, minced garlic, and all the dry spices. Blend with a hand-mixer or blender until smooth.

2 Peel and devein the shrimp (for step by step instructions on Cleaning Shrimp, go to pg. 88). Add them to the citrus marinade and place in the fridge to let the sauce brighten up the shrimp (no more than 3 hours).

3 When you're ready to rock, bring the shrimp out of the fridge and let them come to room temperature while you get your grill up to High Heat.

4 Remove the shrimp from the marinade and shake off any excess sauce. Grill for 1 ½ -2 mins a side – doesn't take long.

5 Heat the tortillas in a hot pan or directly over the burners until warm but still soft. Don't let them get crunchy or burn. Place a layer of shredded cabbage (or better yet, **Mexican Cabbage Salsa** or **Curtido**) in the middle of each tortilla as the base. Add the shrimp and drizzle with **Crema-verde Dipping Sauce** or **Green Onion Aioli**. Serve with lime wedges.

CREMA-VERDE DIPPING SAUCE

Ever whipped up a quesadilla or taco at or after midnight? This dipping sauce came from one such occasion and the subsequent fridge scavenging that followed. Who knew that such an easy and tasty sauce existed on the condiment shelf in the fridge?

Raiding Results:
1/4 cup Mexican Crema (sour cream)
1/8 cup green taco sauce
2 Tbs juice from a jar of pickled jalapenos
1/2 tsp onion powder
1/2 tsp garlic salt

1 Whisk all ingredients together. The longer it rests in the fridge the more the flavors will party and pop.

GREEN ONION AIOLI

Green Onion. Scallions. Spring Onions. Salad Onions. Since I'm not a biologist, and I don't spend my time researching the Allium Genus, po-*tay*-toh, puh-*tah*-toh. This sauce is both earthy and citrusy and is great drizzled on **Grilled Citrus-Shrimp Tacos** or served as a dipping sauce with lamb or steak.

Booker T's Track List:
8-10 green onions
olive oil
pinch of garlic salt
4 Tbs mayo
2 Tbs lemon juice (1 lemon)
1 Tbs sour cream
1 tsp minced garlic
1/8 tsp coarse ground salt

1 Sprinkle the green onions with olive oil and garlic salt. Char by grilling over Medium-High flames or place under the broiler in your oven (at least 6 inches below the flames). Cook for 4-5 mins, flip, and cook the other side for 4-5 mins. Keep an eye on them to make sure they don't blast past char and straight into burn-ville. Remove from the heat and let cool.

2 Mix together the mayo, lemon juice, sour cream, garlic, and salt.

3 Remove the root-ends off each onion and then slice into small chunks. Add to the mayo mixture and blend until smooth. This sauce seems to get better the longer the ingredients have time to mingle and get to know one another so I like to make it a day or two ahead of time.

TOMATILLO SALSA VERDE

Ever had a pot-luck at Work? Unless you've worked in an Emergency Telecommunications Dispatch Center, you haven't experienced all that a pot-luck can be. Working 12-hour shifts, that quickly become 18-hour shifts (thanks to mandatory OT), in one of the world's most demanding and stressful jobs, leads to some pro-level grazing. This delicious tomatillo salsa manages to be sweet, savory, salty, and a little spicy – kind of like the dispatchers I worked with. Thanks to GR for sharing the inspiration for this awesome recipe. Now I can have pot-lucks at home – and without the Mandation.

PSAP Pals:
1/2 lb tomatillos
2-4 jalapenos
1/2 cup diced yellow onion
1/2 cup chopped cilantro
1/4 cup diced green onions (4 stalks)
juice of 1 lime
1 Tbs minced garlic
1 Tbs coarse ground salt
2 tsp onion powder
1/4 – 1/3 cup of water
1 avocado

1 Remove the husk and stem from each tomatillo and discard. Add the tomatillos to a pot of room temperature water and blanch over Medium Heat. Cook them until they just start to get soft – don't let them get mushy (about 10 mins).

2 Remove from the pot and place them in a bowl of ice water to cool.

3 Place the jalapenos on the grill or on the burner of a gas stove. Slightly char all sides. Depending on the size and heat level of the jalapenos, use 2 or 3 (4 if you like it caliente). When charred, remove the stem and rough chop. Add to the blender.

4 Chop the yellow onion, cilantro, and green onions, and add them to the blender. When the tomatillos have cooled down, chop them up and add them to the blender too.

5 Squeeze in the juice of one lime, add the minced garlic, salt, and onion powder.

6 Remove the skin and pit from the avocado. Add half of the avocado to the blender. Pour in 1/4 – 1/3 cup of water just to help the ingredients blend. Give the blender a few pulses to bring everything together. The salsa should be chunky. Don't ride the blender's highest setting or you'll wind up making tomatillo soup.

7 Place in the fridge to let everything siesta for at least 2 hours. Before serving, dice the second half of the avocado and stir into the salsa. Serve with tortilla chips or pour this over your favorite tacos.

MEXICAN CABBAGE SALSA

If there's one thing I learned from my time in the Central Valley, it's that when you sit down at a Mexican Restaurant, you should have more than just a bowl of tortilla chips and blended salsa brought out as an appetizer. This Mexican Cabbage Salsa brings a crisp, refreshing crunch to scoop your chips into. Don't know why this isn't a staple at all Mexican Restaurants – but it is my standard by which I now judge them.

• makes about 3 cups •

Chip Dips:
2 cups diced green cabbage
3 Roma tomatoes, seeded and diced
1/4 cup chopped cilantro leaves
1/4 cup diced onion
1/8 cup diced pickled jalapenos
juice of 1 lime
1 tsp coarse ground salt

1 Dice the green cabbage into small chunks.

2 Slice the Roma tomatoes in half lengthwise. With a spoon or small knife, scrape out the seeds and discard. Dice into small chunks.

3 Pull the cilantro leaves from the main stem (okay to use the smaller stems). Run a knife across them once or twice to give them a rough chop.

4 Dice the onion and the pickled jalapenos.

5 Add all of the diced veggies and cilantro into a large bowl. Add the juice of one lime and the salt. Mix everything together and get to scooping.

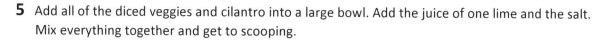 (K+) You can buy pre-chopped or shredded cabbage (often sold as coleslaw) to save some prep time.

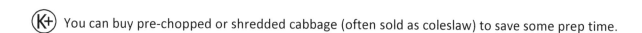 Leftover cabbage? Then time to make some **Creamy Cool-Slaw**.

CURTIDO

This Salvadoran cabbage slaw is usually paired with the delicious dish Pupusas. It should be paired with everything. This is a great side dish for tacos, quesadillas, or nachos, but is also delicious with pork tenderloin, grilled chops, or even fried chicken as the vinegar provides a nice balance to the fry.

San Salvador Slaw Supplies:
juice of 1 lime
1/4 cup apple cider vinegar
1 tsp sugar
1 tsp dried Mexican Oregano
1/4 tsp of red pepper flakes
1/4 tsp coarse ground salt
1 ½ cups finely sliced cabbage
1/4 cup finely sliced onion
1/4 cup finely sliced carrots

1 Mix the juice of one lime with the apple cider vinegar. Whisk in the sugar until it is dissolved. Then mix in the Mexican Oregano, red pepper flakes, and salt.

> Yes, you have to use Mexican Oregano. Traditional (Greek) dried oregano is one of my favorite spices, and I love the earthy flavor it brings to meat and vinaigrettes, but Mexican Oregano brings a sweeter gift to the party. Cabbage and carrots aren't expensive so splurge on some good dried spices so you can make this dish right.

2 Shred or finely slice the cabbage, onions, and the carrots.

3 Combine the veggies and the vinegar sauce. If you are able to let this sit in the fridge overnight to marinate, then you have more willpower than I do. But at least try to give it 4 hours so the lime and vinegar have a chance to soften the cabbage and carrots. Good luck waiting that long. May the odds ever be in your favor.

SHRIMP

On the bus to Basic Training I sat down next to a fellow recruit named Benjamin Buford Blue. Bubba, to his friends, was from Bayou La Batre in Alabama and aspired to be a shrimp boat captain. His family knew everything there is to know about the shrimping business. He told me that shrimp is the fruit of the sea. You can barbecue it, boil it, broil it, bake it, sauté it. There's shrimp kabobs, shrimp creole, shrimp gumbo. Shrimp pan fried, deep fried, stir-fried. There's pineapple shrimp, lemon shrimp, coconut shrimp, pepper shrimp, shrimp soup, shrimp stew, shrimp salad, shrimp and potatoes, shrimp burger, shrimp sandwich. And that's about it.

So yeah, shrimp is both delicious and versatile. Like I always say, shrimp is as shrimp does.

BUYING SHRIMP

The size of shrimp is measured by how many are contained in one pound. "21-25s" are average sized shrimp as there are between 21 and 25 in a pound. "16-20s" are larger as it takes fewer of them to reach a pound. Both "21-25s" and "16-20s" are good, affordable options for most recipes. For grilling, and when it's time to spend a little more money on a meatier shrimp, "13-15s" are preferable. To really splurge, try "4-6s". They might cost a kidney but I think they taste better than lobster. Try them once and you'll want them all the time. Besides, you have two kidneys.

Shrimp is also sold by 'unit' number. So U20 means that there will be no more than 20 shrimp in a pound. Restaurants sometimes advertise shrimp by using the word "jumbo". This is misleading as the use of this word rarely has anything to do with the size of the shrimp. It's a subjective superlative, like when I refer to myself as super-wicked smart and witty.

Other than live shrimp, between raw and cooked, always buy raw. Cooked shrimp tastes like a wet sponge. If you like shrimp cocktail, then buy raw shrimp and make your own shrimp cocktail. Also, buy shrimp that is still in the shell. Shell = Flavor.

Lastly, if you are not able to validate that the shrimp you are buying from the market is fresh, buy frozen. Most generic-type grocery markets will place a pile of shrimp on crushed ice and garnish with parsley and lemon-halves to entice you into buying "fresh" shrimp. But whatever shrimp is not purchased that day, or in a few days, just gets rotated to the bottom of the pile. Never be afraid to ask to smell the shrimp – or any seafood for that matter. The nose knows. You can also check the shell. It should be firmly attached. If the shell is thin or falling off, the shrimp is not fresh. If there is any doubt, pre-packaged frozen shrimp is available in a range of sizes. I like to keep a bag of "16-20s" and "13-15s" in my freezer at all times. They thaw quickly and are a life-saver on those nights when you don't have anything planned for dinner and need a tasty and easy "go-to" meal.

TYPES OF SHRIMP

There's Wild versus Farmed. Saltwater vs. Freshwater. Cold water vs. Warm water. Pink, White, Brown, Spotted, Striped, etc. The primary rule of thumb is to purchase what you have access to provided it is good quality and within your budget.

- White Shrimp and Pink Shrimp are the most common and have the most recognizable shrimp flavor. They are tender and sweet. They take seasoning well and hold up across all mediums of cooking.

- Tiger Prawns have a fuller seafood flavor and are firm and grill well. If you like the taste of shrimp and aren't going to over-season or add sauces, this is a good shrimp to use.

- Whole (head on) Spot Prawns (if you can find them) are freakin' awesome. But cha-ching $$$.

A common joke in the restaurant industry goes: *"What's the difference between shrimp and prawns?..... $2.99 a pound!"* The word "prawn" seems decadent and just reads better off a menu. So why not engage the wordsmithing of a White House Press Secretary to spin "boiled shrimp served with lemon" into "Cocktailed Prawn Sous Vide avec Citrus Accoutrements". You're still getting Shrimp Cocktail but you're going to pay a lot more for it. (There are anatomical differences between a prawn and a shrimp, but unless you plan on going onto a Game Show, this anecdotal trivia doesn't impact your ability to buy and cook the required seafood for any of the recipes in this book.)

CLEANING SHRIMP

When cooking on the grill I prefer to keep the shrimp in the shell as it imparts flavor (and prevents the meat from sticking to the hot grates). When a recipe does call for peeled shrimp, it's classy presentation to leave the last section of shell with the tail intact.

Next, the shrimp should be "deveined". (Since I'm not a carcinologist, I'll refer to these less than appealing parts of the shrimp as "veins".) There are lots of custom-made tools and kitchen utensils marketed for the mono-use of "deveining" shrimp. Save your money. A flat-edged (non-serrated) knife or pair of scissors will work just fine. If you are leaving the shell on, you can make a small incision across the back of the shrimp from the open (fatter) end down to just above the tail. This "butterfly" cut allows you access to the "vein" while leaving the shell in place on either side of the shrimp. When removing the shell, you can also make a small incision on the underside of the shrimp to remove this "vein" as well. It's not required but does make for a very clean and visually appealing crustacean.

NAKED SHRIMP

The best Christmas present I ever got was a surprise visit from our granddaughter. The most enjoyable gifts aren't the ones that cost the most money or are the fanciest. The fact that she showed up, unexpected, created a memory that is better than anything that could have been bought and wrapped. Later, when we celebrated with our holiday feast, Lilly asked for some naked shrimp. Makes perfect sense. Shrimp cocktail just chill without wearing their shells, they're not the fanciest shrimp dish, and the deliciousness of such a simple appetizer is unexpected and always something special.

The Well:
1 pound of shrimp
   (16-20s or 13-15s)
2 Tbs Old Bay Seasoning
1 Tbs coarse ground salt
1 bay leaf
1 lemon

The Cocktail:
1/4 cup ketchup
1 tsp lemon juice
1 tsp Worcestershire Sauce
1 tsp horseradish

1 Shrimp boiled in water tastes like water. So go Top Shelf and make your shrimp cocktail in shrimp stock. Shrimp boiled in shrimp stock tastes like champagne-diamonds-rainbow-shooting-star shrimp.

2 Place a metal bowl or a metal pot in the freezer so that it has time to chill and frost over. You'll need this later.

3 Peel and de-vein the shrimp. (**Cleaning Shrimp**, pg. 88) Place the shrimp in the fridge for now and place the shells into a pot.

4 Fill the pot with 1/2 gallon (8 cups) of cold water. Add the Old Bay seasoning, salt, and bay leaf. Bring to a boil over High Heat and then turn down to Medium and simmer for 60-90 mins to reduce by a quarter to a third of the original volume.

5 While waiting for the stock to reduce, make the Cocktail Sauce. Mix the ketchup, lemon juice, Worcestershire Sauce and horseradish and chill in the fridge until the shrimp are ready. For extra "spicy" sauce add more horseradish.

6 When the stock is reduced, remove the shrimp from the fridge and let them warm up to room temperature.

7 Once the stock is to your liking, turn off the heat. Drop the shrimp in and give them a quick stir to make sure they are completely submerged. They are going to cook quick so set a timer or keep an eye on a clock. For 16-20s, you'll remove them from the stock after 90 seconds. For 13-15s, fish them out after 2 mins.

8 Remember that metal bowl/pot you placed into your freezer? This is what you'll put the shrimp in after you remove them from their quick dip in the stock. The cold bowl/pot will help shock them and stop them from over cooking so that they are nice and tender and not overly-chewy rubber. In place of using an ice bath for the shocking, a frozen metal bowl/pot will not wash out the stock flavor or water down the shrimp.

9 Squeeze the juice of half a lemon over the shrimp and move the shrimp around in the frozen bowl/pot to maximize contact with the cold surface and coat in the lemon juice.

10 Place the pot/bowl back in the freezer for 12-15 mins to continue to shock the shrimp. Do not let the shrimp freeze. You want cocktails not shrimp-sicles.

11 Remove the shrimp and serve with lemon wedges and the cocktail sauce.

🔗 Let me kick out another Life Lesson here: it's always better to have too many shrimp than not enough. Leftovers can be applied to **"29 Razor" Remoulade.**

"29 RAZOR" REMOULADE

Creole food in Wisconsin? Yep. You betcha. While not a popular or common cuisine prior to January 26th, 1997; creole, Cajun, or anything Louisiana became nostalgic after the Packers defeated the Patriots in Super Bowl XXXI. While I lived in New Orleans briefly, the first time I had Shrimp Remoulade was actually in Wisconsin. This creamy, mayo-based sauce need not be spicy, but it is a game-winning marinade for shrimp – from 4 to 84 (if you're following my reference). So check off to this play and score.

Audibles:
1 lb of shrimp (13-15s or 16-20s)
1/4 cup finely diced celery
1 Tbs finely diced green onion
1/2 cup mayo
2 Tbs ketchup
1 Tbs lemon juice
  (about 1/2 a lemon)
1 Tbs horseradish
1 tsp Worcestershire Sauce
1 Tbs fresh Italian parsley
  (or 1 tsp dried parsley)
1 tsp minced garlic
1 tsp cayenne (1/2 tsp for mild)
1/2 tsp celery salt
1/2 tsp paprika
1/2 tsp coarse ground salt

1 Bring a pot of salted water to a boil. Add the shrimp, deveined but with the shell still on. (**Cleaning Shrimp**, pg. 88) Turn the heat off and let the shrimp cook through for two minutes. Remove them from the water and set aside to drain.

2 Dice the celery and green onion as small as you can.

3 Whisk the mayo, ketchup, lemon juice, horseradish, and Worcestershire Sauce together. Add all of the remaining players and bring the team together.

4 Peel the shrimp (retaining the tail for presentation) and add them to the sauce. Work them through to get them coated in the deliciousness. Marinate in the fridge for at least 4 hours up to overnight.

5 Serve as an appetizer, side dish, or even as a salad on top of your favorite greens.

44.501537, -88.060174

NOLA BBQ SHRIMP

Do you have a Bucket List? If going to New Orleans and eating BBQ Shrimp is not on your list, throw it out. Your Bucket List need only have this one item on it. The following recipe sucks. It is a weak attempt at duplicating something that cannot be duplicated outside of the Crescent City. While fresh shrimp can now be obtained from a number of purveyors across the country, there is no French Bread anywhere in the world that compares to what is baked in the shadow of the lower Mississippi River. Dunking sliced Wonder Bread into this buttery nectar of the Gulf-Coast Gods is an affront to all culinary humanity, but in a pinch, use whatever baguette you can find. So I guess this lame-ass recipe will have to suffice.

Packing List:
1 lb shrimp (13-15s are best)
  deveined, but shell on
  (**Cleaning Shrimp** pg. 88)
1/4 cup diced celery
1/4 cup diced yellow onion
6 Tbs unsalted butter
1/2 Tbs minced garlic
1/2 lemon
4 Tbs Worcestershire Sauce
1/2 Tbs hot sauce
1/2 Tbs coarse ground salt
1/2 tsp black pepper
1 tsp dried rosemary
1 tsp dried parsley
1/2 tsp paprika
green onion as garnish
French bread

1 Choppity-chop the celery and onion.

2 Heat a pan over Medium Heat. Add 1 Tbs butter and then sauté the celery and onion until soft (5-6 mins).

3 Turn the heat down to Low and add the garlic. Squeeze in the juice of the lemon and cook for 2 mins, stirring frequently to prevent the garlic from burning. (set aside the lemon after squeezing out the juice)

4 Stir in the Worcestershire Sauce, hot sauce, and all of the dry spices. Take the lemon you set aside and slice off 2-3 thin slices. Drop these into the pan. Simmer everything for 4-5 mins to incorporate the flavors.

5 Add the shrimp and cook for 4-5 mins. Stir in the remaining butter, 1 Tbs at a time, stirring until each one is melted before adding the next one. Turn off the heat and let the shrimp take a short spa break while you slice the baguette and work up an ice-cold Mint Julip. Letting them just hang out in the pool for 8-10 mins will allow them to absorb more of the buttery BBQ sauce.

6 Serve the shrimp in a deep bowl with the sauce so that you can dip the bread.

BOOM-STICK BUFFALO SHRIMP

This shrimp packs a punch. If you're a primitive screwhead that's afraid of spicy food, don't you worry. The buttery cream sauce makes this sweet baby a dish you'll be able to handle. So say the words: *"Klaatu"*, *"Barada"*,... um, ..., *"Creamy-Buffalo-Wing-Sauce-Simmered Shrimp"*. You got that? Groovy.

• 2-3 servings •

Shop S-Mart:
1 lb shrimp (16-20s or 21-25s)
1/2 cup hot sauce (a cayenne-pepper
    sauce like Frank's Original RedHot)
6 Tbs unsalted butter (cold)
1/2 cup heavy cream
salt and black pepper to taste

1 Peel and devein the shrimp.
(**Cleaning Shrimp** pg. 88)

2 Warm the hot sauce in a pan over
Low Heat for 4-5 minutes.

3 Stir in the cold butter, 1 Tbs at a time, stirring constantly to prevent the sauce from breaking. When the first Tbs is melted, then add the next one, stirring constantly, until it is dissolved into the sauce. Repeat until you have added all of the butter. If your wrist gets tired from whisking, then you're doing it right.

4 While stirring constantly, slowly pour in the cream and keep stirring until it is mixed thoroughly into the sauce. Simmer for 4-5 mins.

5 Season the shrimp with salt and black pepper and then add to the sauce. Depending on the size of your pan, if the shrimp are completely submerged in the sauce, cook for 5 mins over Low Heat. If the pan is large, and the shrimp are not submerged, cook for 3 mins, flip, and then cook the opposite side for 3 mins.

6 Remove the shrimp from the sauce and place them into a large bowl. Pour the sauce over the top and then serve with some good crunchy bread for dipping. Yeah, the shrimp are good, but really, it's all about the bread dunking.

(Tips) Shrimp live in water. So they're kinda watery. After you clean them, give each one a light squeeze, or some paper towel hugs, to get some of the moisture out. This will help them absorb more of the sauce – like a sponge. A tasty, tasty, shrimp sponge.

SHRIMP TWO-O-NINE

Our version of "Family Night" was sitting around the table peeling shrimp, dipping them into the buttery chili-lime sauce, enjoying some carbonated beverages, and of course, each other's company. When we were fortunate enough to all live in the same Area Code, having the "kids" (they are grown now) over for a Friday Night shrimp feast was the highlight of the week. Good memories. Now when I make this shrimp, I have to mail it to the kids. Is it weird that they mail the empty shells back to me?

1 Devein the shrimp but leave the shell on. (**Cleaning Shrimp**, pg. 88)

2 Get your grill fired up to High Heat. Place the shrimp over the hottest part of the grill and cook for 90 seconds to 2 mins a side – just long enough to get some good char on the shells. Remove from the heat and place in a large bowl while you make the sauce. (Alternatively, you can char these under the broiler in your oven for 2 mins a side.)

3 In a saucepan, heat the lime juice over Low Heat. Whisk in the chili powder, smoked paprika, salt, and garlic powder.

4 After the sauce warms up, add 1 Tbs of cold butter and whisk continually until it melts. Add another Tbs of butter and whisk until melted. Repeat until all the butter has been whisked into sauce. (To keep the sauce from breaking keep the heat Low, the butter cold, and never stop whisking.)

5 Pour the sauce over the shrimp and let them sop up the flavor for a couple minutes before serving (6-8 mins). This will leave you enough time to enjoy your choice of ice-cold carbonated beverage.

• 1/2 lb of shrimp per person •

Meaningful Memories:
1 lb of shrimp (16-20s)
1/4 cup lime juice
   (2 limes)
1/2 Tbs chili powder
1/2 Tbs smoked paprika
1/2 Tbs coarse ground salt
1 tsp garlic powder
1 stick (8 Tbs) of unsalted
   butter (cold)

37.663241, -120.653548

MANGO-HABANERO SHRIMP SKEWERS

Whenever I think of shrimp skewers sizzling over a hot fire, I feel like I should be in Australia sinking a slab of XXXX Gold and sweating over the barbie. I used to work for a tour company that specialized in motor-coach trips across the United States where the clients were primarily from Australia. After a season on the road with some true-blue mates, I picked up some of the Aussie strine. So if you're wondering if these sweet-hot prawns are bloody good tucker, they're aces. Fair dinkum. Give it a burl and bog in. There's an optional recipe for a dipping sauce that is choc-a-bloc of flavor. (If you're a bogan that dips everything in dead horse, then you need to read the chapter on **The World's Worst Food**.)

• makes 12 oz of sauce •
(6 oz of sauce is good
for a pound of 16-20s)

Proper Prawn Party:
1 lb shrimp (13-15s or 16-20s)
1 mango
1/4 cup diced habaneros
    (3-4 small peppers)
1 cup sugar
1/2 cup water
1/2 cup white vinegar
1 tsp table salt

Optional Sauce:
    2 Tbs sour cream
    coarse ground salt

1 Slice the mango away from the pit and scrape the meat from the skin. Chop into small chunks and add the fruit to a saucepan.

2 Remove the stems from the habanero peppers and finely dice. Add to the mango in the pan.

3 Over Medium Heat, cook the mango and the habaneros for 4-5 minutes to soften them up and give them some exposure to the hot pan. Stir occasionally but be careful about leaning over the pan unless you need a good cry.

 Make the sauce on your grill – outside. This will keep you from having to don your M40 FPM in your kitchen for the rest of the day.

4 Add the rest of the ingredients and stir until the sugar dissolves.
Using a hand mixer or a blender, bring the ingredients together and mix/blend until the consistency is smooth. (If you're using a blender, and adding the sauce when it is still hot, make sure the lid is firmly attached – AND push down on the lid with one hand as you work the blender through its LOWEST setting. Hot liquid + blender + loose lid or highest setting = fun trip to the Urgent Care Clinic to get your eyeballs washed out (16-A-1 for those in the know).

5 Once the sauce is smooth, simmer over Low Heat for 8-10 mins until it thickens to your liking. While it's coming together, devein the shrimp but leave the shell on. (**Cleaning Shrimp** pg. 88)

6 Let the sauce cool and then pour it over the deveined shrimp and place in the fridge to marinate for an hour.

7 If using wooden skewers, soak them in water for an hour so that they don't immediately catch on fire as soon as you place them on the hot grill. Place 4-5 shrimp on each skewer and then grill them over Medium-High Heat for 2 mins a side.

8 Remove from the grill and sprinkle with the coarse ground salt before serving.

 Dipping Sauce: Mix the 2 Tbs of sour cream with 1 Tbs of the Mango-Habanero Sauce and a pinch of coarse ground salt. Stir together and serve with the shrimp skewers.

 This is the same marinade used for the **Balrog Fire Wings**. If you have any sauce leftover, make some wings.

INTERESTING EVENTS
IN ALCOHOL HISTORY

Charles II of Navarre, also known as Charles the Bad, was a King during the Hundred Years' War. In addition to assassinating political opponents, massacring French revolutionaries, and making and breaking secret deals with rival leaders to further his own ambition, he once directed that all of the prisoners be released from the prisons in Paris to create chaos and discourse. Later in his life, when he fell ill, his physician recommended a treatment that involved being wrapped in blankets infused with brandy. After his servants had sewn him into his bed, under brandy-soaked sheets, a candle accidentally set the brandy, and the sheets, and the King, on fire. Charles the Bad was burned alive in his own bed.

Alcohol must be labeled with its volume by percentage, or ABV (Alcohol By Volume). This is often referred to as "Proof". This is a carryover from the days when the British Royal Navy provided its sailors a daily ration of rum. The sailors wanted proof that the rum was not watered down so they'd add a pinch of gunpower and light it on fire. If the wet gunpowder didn't ignite, it was an indication that the rum was watered down. If the gunpowder flashed in the rum, this indicated that the alcohol by volume was at least 57% and proved that their daily ration of rum was the real deal.

The first Federal Tax in the newly formed United States of America was a liquor tax, where the money collected would be used to pay down the debts incurred during the War for Independence. While the distilleries in the major cities of the East Coast could afford this tax, the pioneers in the West were making liquor on a smaller scale – and often for their own consumption or to use for trade and bartering. This was particularly true in western Pennsylvania where they rebelled against paying this tax. When the tax collection turned violent, the government sent troops, led by President George Washington himself. While the 'Whiskey Rebellion' was quelled, this event led many distillers to migrate further west into the frontier (what is present day Tennessee and Kentucky – which is why the influence of whiskey and distilleries are so strong in both States today). The Whiskey Rebellion was also a catalyst for starting the Republican Political Party (but that's a story for another time and book).

In 2007, a conservation team from New Zealand was making repairs to a small building in Antarctica that was built by Sir Ernest Shackleton in 1907 during his expedition to the South Pole. They discovered a crate of Scotch Whiskey under the floorboards. Several bottles of Scotch were still intact and unopened. These bottles of Mackinlay's Rare Old Highland Malt were part of a special order Shackleton had requested from the distillery specifically for his expedition and dated back to a vintage from 1896. As this brand of Scotch is no longer made, a few bottles were carefully thawed and sent to Scotland for analysis. From the small samples taken, master distillers were able to recreate the original recipe from over 100 years ago.

When the British East India Company expanded British influence around the globe, they were exposed to tropical climates – and the diseases that were common in these parts of the world. Malaria took many lives until it was discovered that quinine could be used as a treatment. In the 1800s, during the British incursion of India, the soldiers were issued a daily dose of quinine. On its own, this is extremely bitter. To make their daily doses more palatable, they began mixing the quinine with soda water, and then sugar. This soon became known as Indian Tonic. To make the quinine tonic even easier to keep down, sailors began adding lime juice. Limes were a common import item so they were frequently on the East India Company's ships – and may have also been prescribed to the sailors as a prophylaxis for scurvy. Being British, there was also no shortage of gin available. And this was the last piece of the puzzle to create what we now know as the delicious and refreshing 'Gin & Tonic'.

There is an island off the coast of Greenland that is claimed by both the Danes and the Canadians. Hans Island is a frozen, uninhabited, chunk of rock in the Nares Strait. In 1984, the Danish Minister of Greenland erected the Flag of Denmark on the island with a welcome sign and a bottle of schnapps. Subsequently, the Canadians raised their own flag, left their own welcome sign, and replaced the bottle of schnapps with a bottle of Canadian Whiskey. This conflict-less conflict between these two countries has continued for the last 40 years.

In 1953, British author Ian Fleming created the character James Bond with his first book, 'Casino Royal'. In addition to creating the famous British Spy "007", he also invented the cocktail "Vesper".

"Three measures of Gordon's, one of vodka, half a measure of Kina Lillet. Shake it very well until it's ice-cold, then add a large slice of lemon-peel. Got it?"

While James Bond may have created this cocktail, he never ordered it, or drank one, in any of the subsequent novels. Was it because it was named after the woman he loved – who wound up being a Soviet Intelligence asset and then broke his heart? Or was it because it really wasn't that tasty of a cocktail? Regardless, from that moment on, James Bond drank champagne, Scotch and soda, and gin martinis. But the drink made famous by this fictional character, was the Vodka Martini – "shaken, not stirred"

98

SEAFOOD

There is something luxurious about the foods that come from our rivers and oceans. Whether high-priced items on restaurant menus or the desired station at buffets, seafood elevates the experience. But it need not be intimidating. These recipes are simple dishes that you're sure to quickly master and enjoy.

WILD SALMON WITH LEEK CREAM SAUCE

Leeks don't seem to be the most popular vegetable but they should be. Part onion, part garlic, all tasty. Simmering them down into a sauce makes for a sweet and creamy topping that also adds some crunch. This is a great balance to seafood – especially salmon.

Resist the temptation to save money by purchasing farmed salmon. Go wild. In addition to supporting the Fishing Industry, the extra dollars you spend equate to better flavor and a healthier, happier fish. And don't you want your fish to be happy?

Copper River Run:

4 wild salmon filets
2 cups leeks, sliced
1 cup heavy cream
1 tsp coarse ground salt
1/4 tsp black pepper
2 Tbs unsalted butter
olive oil

1 Slice the root-end off of the leek and discard. Remove the top inch of the dark green end. Cut the leek in half lengthwise from the white root-end to the green leafend. Separate each layer and rinse under cold water to remove the residual dirt. Set aside on a towel to dry.

2 In a pan over Medium-Low Heat, simmer the cream, salt, and black pepper for 2-3 mins. Add the butter and stir continually until it melts. Once melted, simmer for 5 mins.

3 Slice the leeks (the whites and the greens) into 1/4-inch slices. Add them to the sauce and cook for 8-10 mins, stirring occasionally.

4 Heat a second pan over Medium Heat and add just enough olive oil to coat the bottom. Wait for the oil to come to temperature (1-2 mins). Add the salmon. (If the salmon still has the skin on it, you can either remove it if you have Food Network knife skills, or just cook it with the skin on and remove the skin after it's cooked. In this case, start cooking the salmon skin-side down and add 1 extra minute of cook time to this side.)

5 Cook the salmon until you see them heating through (changing color) halfway up the thickest part of the filet. If the salmon is 1/2-inch to 3/4-inch thick, you'll only need about 3 mins on the first side. Flip the salmon and cook the second (or non-skin side) for 2-3 mins. For 1-inch filets: 5 mins, flip, 3-4 mins.

6 Remove from the pan and plate. Spoon the leek sauce over the top (as much or as little as you desire). Serve with lemon wedges and some tasty bread for the obligatory sauce-sopping.

SAN FRAN BEER CLAMS

Growing up in a State that didn't border either ocean, clams were always fried, served in newspaper, and dipped in cocktail sauce. It wasn't until I spent some time in North Beach that I saw and experienced all a clam could be. My first garlic & clam pizza on Broadway and Columbus was, as they say in Northern California, "hell'ah good". They fueled my fire to explore every item on the menus of Little Italy's restaurants. This recipe is quick, delicious, easy, and delicious. Delicious deserves double-mention as who doesn't love beer and butter?

Bay Area Bivalves:
1 lb clams (unless you live in
   New England, plan on 10 per lb)
1/2 gallon of tap water
1/6 cup sea salt
1 stick unsalted butter (8 Tbs)
1/2 Tbs chopped garlic
1/2 tsp coarse ground salt
1/3 of a bottle of beer (4oz)
   (go SF style and use Anchor Steam)

1 Check each clam and discard any that have broken shells or shells that will not close when handled or tapped. Wash the remaining shells in tap water and scrub off any sand or dirt.

2 Fill a large pot, or your sink, with a 1/2 gallon of water and 1/6 cup of sea salt (don't use table salt) per pound of clams. Submerge the clams in the salt water for at least an hour for them to purge the sand from inside their shells.

3 After the clams have been cleaned, melt the butter in a pan over Medium Heat. Add the garlic and 1/2 tsp of coarse ground salt. Simmer for 3-4 mins.

4 Stir in the beer (1/3 bottle / 4 oz). Remove the clams from the salt water and give them once last rinse under tap water before adding to the party.

5 Cover and turn the heat down to Low. Simmer until all of the clams open up (about 12 mins). 12 whole minutes? Boring. Ya know what you can do in 12 minutes? Drink the other two-thirds of that delicious beer.

6 Pour the clams – and the sauce – into a deep-bottomed dish or bowl. Serve with warm sourdough bread so you can soak up all of the buttery, beer, clam-liquor sauce.

 Add shrimp to the mix. After the clams are done, cook the shrimp for 5 mins (or 3 mins a side if not submerged).

QA WINE MUSSELS

QA. The acronym for Quality Assurance. As both my wife and I work in QA, we're focused on quality management and the review of systems, protocols, and providing service. As it's human-nature for people to deviate from structure, scripting, and standardization, we're also experienced with drinking wine and banging our heads against the table when dispatchers don't "read it as written".

This mussels-classic is super easy to simmer up but you want to make sure that you're starting with a quality product. Don't cut corners or lower your standards. Even if you have a trusted monger that you rely on, you should always check your mussels before cooking. If a shell is cracked, then it's no good. If the shell is broken, no good. If the shell won't close when you tap on it, no good. And for a dish as tasty as this one, you want all your clams to pass their quality review.

Quality Control Checklist:

1 lb mussels
4 Tbs unsalted butter
1/2 cup white wine
 (a good buttery chardonnay)
1/2 tsp coarse ground salt
pasta and/or French bread

1 Give your mussels the freshness inspection and then give them a rinse to clean the shells. If there are seaweed looking fibers (known as the beard) hanging out of the shell, use your fingers to pull them out of the mussel.

2 Melt the butter in a pan over Medium Heat. Add the wine and salt and cook for 4-5 mins.

3 Add the mussels and cover the pan. Simmer until the mussels open up (8-10 mins). If there are mussels that haven't opened after 15 minutes, then they haven't passed the test. Remove them and throw them out.

4 Pour the remaining mussels and the beautiful wine sauce into a large bowl. For an appetizer, serve with a good bread for dipping. For a meal, serve with your favorite pasta (linguini is traditional but boil up whatever ya got on hand).

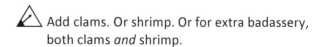 Add clams. Or shrimp. Or for extra badassery, both clams *and* shrimp.

THAI-STYLE MUSSELS & CLAMS

There's something about food from this part of the World that appeals to every taste bud on my tongue. I usually lament the fact that I have to book a flight and navigate airport security just to get a decent Po Boy – but at least this travel is in the same hemisphere. I can't imagine my limited attention span surviving a flight to the other side of the globe. Luckily, there are an increasing number of Laotian, Cambodian, Vietnamese, and Thai restaurants in most North American cities so I don't have to dust off my passport and shoehorn my ass into the smallest and most uncomfortable seat in the air.

These ingredients are a staple and this simple sauce gets used with shrimp, clams, mussels, all three, poured over rice, tossed with noodles, and even drizzled over roasted or grilled corn on the cob.

Boarding Group:
clams (1/2 lb per person)
mussels (1/4 lb per person)
shrimp (4 per person)
1/2 gallon of tap water
   (per lb of clams)
1/6 cup sea salt
   (per lb of clams)
2-inch chunk of fresh ginger
1 shallot
1/4 cup diced cilantro stems
1 lime
1-2 Tbs vegetable oil
1 Tbs minced garlic
1-3 tsp of red curry paste
1 Tbs fish sauce
1 tsp coarse ground salt
1 (15 oz) can of coconut milk

1 To prepare and clean the clams, discard any that have broken shells or shells that will not close when handled. Rinse the shells and scrub off any sand or dirt. Soak the clams in a mixture of tap-water and 1/6 cup sea salt (not table salt) for at least one hour to purge the sand from inside the shells.

2 For the mussels, give them a quick rinse and discard any that have broken shells. If the shells don't close when handled, discard these as well. If there are seaweed looking fibers (known as the beard) hanging out of the shell, use your fingers to pull them out of the mussel.

3 Peel and devein the shrimp (check out pg. 88 for instructions on **Cleaning Shrimp**).

4 Peel the ginger and cut (along the grain of the ginger) into two 1/4-inch slices. Cut the ends off the shallot and remove the first papery layer and discard. Dice the remaining layers. Dice 1/4 cup of cilantro stems. With a micro-plane, or some ninja knife work, zest half a lime.

5 Warm a large pan over Medium Heat. Add a couple Tbs of vegetable oil. Add the ginger, shallot, garlic, cilantro stems, and lime zest. Sauté for 4-5 mins, stirring to keep the garlic from burning.

6 Stir in the red curry paste. (1 tsp for mild, 2 for medium, 3 for some heat)

7 Add the fish sauce, the juice of the half a lime you zested, and the coarse ground salt. Then stir in the coconut milk. Simmer for 5-6 mins, stirring occasionally.

8 After the clams have purged, remove them from the salt water and give them a quick rinse. Drop the clams and mussels into the pool and turn the heat down to Low. Cover the pan and cook for 10 mins until the shells open. (If any mussels do not open after 15 mins, remove and discard).

9 When the clams and mussels are cooked (the shells have opened up), add the shrimp. Cook uncovered for 5 mins. (If the shrimp are not submerged in the sauce, flip after 3 mins so each side gets some love.)

10 Pour everything into a large bowl and garnish with cilantro leaves and lime wedges.

> This is a similar sauce to the **Thai-Style Corn on the Cob**.
> So if you have extra sauce left over from one recipe, you can use it for the other.

RELEASE THE KRAKEN

It's disappointing that octopus isn't more popular here in The States. While octopus may seem intimating, it is too delicious to leave out of your culinary repertoire. Like most seafood, it's available pre-cooked and frozen, but is best if you can find it raw and cook it yourself. And it's super easy to cook.

First, find a large rock. Beat the octopus against said rock for 20-30 mins until you get tired. Take a moment to wonder why you are doing this when you are not a Greek Fisherman. Add the poor smashed octopoda to a copper pot of salted water. Ponder why it must be a copper pot considering you are not a Spanish Cook. Add one wine cork for each leg of the octopus. Speculate on the science of this requirement when you are not an Italian Chef. Make sure it is October and the lunar phase is a New Moon. Then, just for giggles, ask yourself if Octopus Recipes are really this difficult and complicated? And the answer is yes. But only according to the internet. If this is your reference, then cooking an octopus is about as challenging as solving the Navier-Stokes equation:

$$\rho[\frac{\partial V}{\partial t}+(V.\nabla)V]=-\nabla P+\rho g+\mu\nabla^2 V$$

Here's a recipe that is more in alignment with my math skills (2nd Grade Level).

1 If not already cleaned by your monger, remove the cartilage and the beak hidden under the head. You don't need a knife or special tools. Just pull them out by hand and discard.

2 Place the raw octopus in a pot and add just enough water (cold to room temperature) to cover.

3 Salt the water heavily and add 1 bay leaf, 2 Tbs Italian Seasoning, and 1 Tbs of minced garlic.

4 Bring to just under a boil over Medium Heat and then turn down to Low Heat. Simmer for 50 mins a pound. It is finished when a knife slides easily into the thickest part (base of the head).

5 When cooked, remove from the water and enjoy in one of the following ways:

GRILLED OCTOPUS

As good as plain 'ole boiled octopus is, adding some fire-char adds both flavor and texture. A quick drizzle of some quality olive oil and aged balsamic makes this one of my favorite dishes. Doesn't get any easier to make so there's really no excuse for you not trying it.

1 Cut each tentacle off and then slice the body/head into large sections.

2 Drizzle with olive oil and let marinate while you fire up your grill as hot as you can get it. A charcoal or wood fire is preferred but propane is always quick and easy.

3 Place the pieces of octopus on the grill and sear each side until they start to darken and crisp a bit. Don't walk away from the fire as these will char up quick (2-3 mins a side).

4 Remove from the grill and plate. Hit them again with a little extra virgin olive oil and a sprinkle of coarse ground sea salt and then drizzle with a nice aged balsamic vinegar.

1983 James Bond Villain:
1 – 1.5 lb cooked octopus
olive oil (your good one)
coarse ground sea salt
aged balsamic vinegar

OCTOPUS SALAD

Memories. Octopus salad reminds me of my childhood, my hometown, and pizza night. The day I figured out that I could make this at home was the happiest day of my life. (Not really the best day I've ever had, but I'm trying to convince you just how good this is. Don't be scared. Try it.) The crunch of the onions and celery provide the perfect balance to the vinaigrette marinated octopus.

Saturday Night Special:
1 – 1.5 lb cooked octopus
1/2 cup extra virgin olive oil
1 Tbs lemon juice (1/2 lemon)
1 tsp coarse ground sea salt
2 tsp dried oregano
1/2 tsp dried parsley
1 cup sliced celery
    (about 2 stalks)
1/2 cup diced yellow onion

1 Whisk together the olive oil, juice of 1/2 lemon, sea salt, dried oregano, and dried parsley.

2 Slice the celery and onion into small chunks (not too finely as the appeal of this salad is the contrasting crunch of the celery and onions). Add to the vinaigrette.

3 Cut the cooked (and cooled) octopus into small chunks and then add to the vinaigrette.

Note: there is a gelatinous skin that some people remove. I prefer to leave this on as I like the flavor and texture it brings to the dish. If it bugs you, wash it off under cold water.

4 Place in the fridge and let all the participants hang out in the vinaigrette-pool for a couple hours (4 hrs to overnight). Let it come to room temperature before eating so the vinaigrette's consistency returns to a dressing and not a gelatin-cube.

 If you want to make this into the childhood meal of my dreams, order a pizza and then make the **68th Street Fried Eggplant**.

PASTA

If variety is the spice of life, then pasta should be eaten every day. So many different kinds, so little time to try them all. But like Yoda says: *"Do, or Do Not. There is no Try."*

MOM'S STUFFED CONCHIGLIE

Growing up, most kids ate vowel-shaped pasta from a can. My brother and I were lucky enough to have a mom that made cheese-stuffed, conch-shell shaped, pasta covered in meat sauce. This dish can be customized with different cheeses, vegetables, meats, and sauces. So after trying this simple and classic recipe, change it up and try your own version. Don't worry, I won't tell my mom.

• 4-5 servings •

Meal Memories:
18-20 jumbo-sized
   shell-shaped pasta
1/2 lb Italian Sausage
2 tsp minced garlic
1 large egg
8 oz ricotta cheese
1 Tbs olive oil
2 tsp dried basil
1 tsp coarse ground salt
1/2 tsp black pepper
1 ½ cups shredded
   mozzarella
24 oz pasta sauce
   (I like marinara)

1 Preheat your oven to 375 degrees. In a pan, sauté the Italian Sausage over Medium Heat on your stovetop until it is browned and cooked through (about 10 mins). While it is cooking, use the side of a spoon to break it up into small chunks. When it's done, stir in the minced garlic and then turn off the heat. Drain (if necessary) and set aside to cool.

2 Make the pasta according to the directions on the box. Maximize your efficiency by making the cheese stuffing while you're waiting for the water to boil and the pasta to cook.

(Tips) Cook a couple extra shells to allow for a few breaking while the pasta cooks or when you stuff them.

3 Whisk the egg and then mix in the ricotta cheese. Add the olive oil, dried basil, salt, black pepper, and 1/2 cup of the shredded mozzarella and stir everything together. Fold in the cooled Italian Sausage.

4 Pour a third of the pasta sauce (1 cup) into a 13 x 9 inch baking dish to coat the bottom. Spoon the cheese mixture into the shells until they are full (about 1 ½ Tbs). Place them in the baking dish and then pour the rest of the pasta sauce (2 cups) over the top.

5 Cover with aluminum foil and bake for 30 minutes. When done, remove the foil, sprinkle the remaining cup of shredded mozzarella over the top and cook uncovered for 2-3 minutes to melt the cheese.

 Try mixing spinach or mushrooms into the cheese stuffing or substitute chicken or ground beef for the sausage.

SHRIMP "I KNOW IT WAS YOU" ALFREDO

Don't go fishing with Al Neri in Lake Tahoe. There's no shrimp in the lake, and even though your younger brother Michael forgave you for betraying him to Hyman Roth, 'Il bacio della morte' should never be taken lightly. But after a long day with "the family", a huge bowl of shrimp fettuccini smothered in 'Fredo sauce is just the thing you need.

• 2 portions •

The 5 Families:
1/2 box fettuccini pasta
4 Tbs unsalted butter
1/2 Tbs minced garlic
1/2 cup heavy cream
1/4 tsp coarse ground salt
1/4 tsp dried oregano
pinch of black pepper
1/2 cup grated parmesan
1/2 cup shredded mozzarella
10-12 shrimp (16-20s or 21-25s),
  peeled and deveined
  (instructions for
  Cleaning Shrimp on pg. 88)

1 Cook the pasta to 'al dente' according to the box instructions.

2 In a large pan, melt the butter over Low Heat and add the garlic. Sauté for 3-4 minutes.

3 Stir in the heavy cream, salt, dried oregano, and black pepper. Simmer, stirring occasionally, for 5 mins.

4 Mix the two cheeses together. Add the cheese a small handful at a time and stir constantly until it melts before adding another handful. This will help keep it smooth and creamy.

5 Add the shrimp and cook in the sauce for 2-3 mins. Flip the shrimp over and cook for another 2 mins.

6 When the pasta is done cooking, strain the water out (or remove with tongs), and add the pasta to the sauce and shrimp. Give them a swirl-n-stir to get the sauce mixed in. Plate and enjoy. Mangia!

 **Gremolata Bread**

(K+) Of course you can buy a jar of alfredo sauce, but it's really easy to make your own and homemade allows you to dial up or down the different flavors to your liking.

BAKED RIGATONI-SOPRANO

Daily Agenda:

- Wake up and walk down your driveway in your bathrobe to get the daily newspaper.

- Read the newspaper as you enjoy a delicious espresso made on the Elektra Microcasa Semiautomatica that Paulie gave you.

- Put in one hour's work in "waste management".

- Sneak out to meet with your therapist, Doctor Melfi.

- Spend the other half of your day at the Bada-Bing with Silvio and your nephew Christopher snacking on gabagool, super-sod, and prujoot.

- Have a delicious dinner of baked rigatoni with Carmela, Meadow, and Anthony Jr.

List of contraband:
olive oil
2 Tbs minced garlic
3/4 lb Italian Sausage
1/2 yellow onion, diced
2 tsp coarse ground salt
6 oz tomato paste
3 (14.5 oz) cans of diced,
   stewed tomatoes
1 Tbs dried oregano
1 Tbs dried thyme
1/2 cup chicken stock
1 lb box of rigatoni pasta
1/2 lb (8 oz) mushrooms,
   sliced
2 cups shredded mozzarella

 Depending on how much you want to make, you'll need an 8x10 or 13x19 oven-safe dish. Since a good sauce takes a few hours to simmer up, I always make more than needed so that I have leftovers. It freezes well and can easily be thawed within the month on some evening when you don't know what to make for dinner. Same with the pasta. Regardless of which size baking dish you're going to use, you'll have some sauce and pasta remaining – so don't try to cram it all into the dish to make it fit. Leftover pasta can be used for other recipes (like the **Hawaiian Mac Salad**) or dried, threaded with yarn, and made into a beautiful necklace like the ones you used to make back in grammar school.

40.8821158,-74.0666921

For the Sauce

1 Heat a pot over Medium Heat. Add 1-2 Tbs of olive oil and let the oil heat up for 1-2 minutes.

2 Add 1 Tbs of the minced garlic and stir for 2-3 minutes taking care that it doesn't burn.

3 Add the Italian Sausage and cook for 8-10 mins to brown. Break the sausage up into small chunks as it cooks. When browned, remove with a slotted spoon and set aside to drain.

4 Add the onion to the pan and 1 tsp of the coarse ground salt. Cook for 4-5 minutes to sweat them down.

5 Add the tomato paste and stir through for 2-3 minutes. Adding the tomato paste directly to the hot pan allows it to caramelize and provides an extra depth of flavor to the finished sauce.

6 Add the stewed tomatoes, dried oregano, thyme, and remaining tsp of salt, and sauté for 10 minutes (stirring every few minutes).

7 Pour in the stock and the remaining 1 Tbs garlic. Adding the garlic at two different points in the recipe provides a layer of garlic flavors. Be a bulb badass.

8 Add the Italian Sausage back in and turn the heat down to Low. Simmer for 2 – 2 ½ hours. (Stir occasionally for the first half of the cook time and more frequently as the sauce begins to thicken to prevent burning.)

For the Pasta

1 Cook the pasta al dente according to the instructions on the box.

2 When done, strain the pasta and set aside.

Bringing it all Together and Baking it Up

1 If using an 8x10 baking dish, add the pasta and pour in 2 cups of the sauce. Add the mushrooms and 1 ½ cups of the shredded mozzarella cheese. Work it all together to get the cheese evenly distributed. (if using a larger dish, increase the amount of sauce and cheese)

2 Cover with aluminum foil and bake for 30 minutes at 375 degrees.

3 Remove the foil, sprinkle the remaining 1/2 cup of mozzarella over the top, and then place back in the oven for 3-4 minutes to melt the cheese.

4 Let sit for 5 minutes before serving.

 Make the sauce ahead of time and then you can bake up the rigatoni on the fly.

 Add black olives, fresh basil, bell peppers, or red chili flakes to add some zip.

PROSTITUTE PASTA

As the old saying goes: *"The way to a man's heart is through his stomach."* Back in the olden days, in Naples, the enterprising businesswomen of the evening took an approach to attracting their customers through their noses. They made a pasta sauce with the most fragrant local ingredients: garlic, anchovies, capers, and olives. While these women were more interested in a man's income than his heart, they still created one of the best sauces in Italy, Puttanesca. You don't need any ulterior motives to simmer this tasty sauce up. It's easy, perfectly legal, and only takes about 20 minutes.

Red Light Aromatics:
olive oil
2 oz tin of anchovy fillets
1 Tbs minced garlic
1/3 cup black olives,
    pitted, sliced
1 ½ Tbs capers
1/2 tsp red pepper flakes
1/2 tsp dried oregano
2 (14.5 oz) cans of stewed,
    diced tomatoes
1/2 box spaghetti

1 Heat a large pan over Medium Heat. Add enough olive oil to coat the bottom of the pan.

2 Add the anchovies and garlic and cook until the anchovies start to dissolve and the garlic browns (about 4-5 mins).

3 Stir in the olives, capers, chili flakes, and dried oregano.

4 Pour the liquid from the stewed tomatoes into the pan and give it a stir. Pour the stewed tomatoes into a large bowl. Break up the tomatoes into small chunks. You can use a knife or a fork, but hands work the best. Just give them a few good squeezes. Add the tomatoes to the pan and simmer for 10 minutes.

5 Cook the pasta al dente according to the box instructions. When done, turn the heat off and add the pasta directly to the sauce with tongs (or a slotted spoon). You don't want to pour all the pasta water into the sauce, but you want whatever water comes with the pasta as the starchy water will help the sauce stick to the spaghetti.

6 Get the party started by stirring the pasta through the sauce. Let them mingle for 2-3 minutes.

7 Serve with garlic bread, or better yet, **Gremolata Bread**.

 Want to score some free red pepper flakes? Order a pizza.

GREMOLATA BREAD

This is a quick and tasty side to accompany meat and seafood dishes. Garlic Bread is a tried and true partner but the lemon zest of gremolata provides a bright balance to meat and seafood. If you need to be "sold" on how much I love gremolata, just flip through the pages of this book to see how many times it's recommended as a side dish.

Ingredienti:
2 Tbs fresh Italian parsley, finely chopped
1/2 Tbs lemon zest
2 Tbs extra virgin olive oil
1/2 Tbs minced garlic
1/4 tsp coarse ground salt
1 baguette of French Bread (or your favorite bread)
unsalted butter

1 Remove the parsley leaves from the main stem (okay to have the little thin stems). Chop finely.

2 With a microplane or zester, "shave" 1/2 Tbs of the yellow peel off of the lemon. Do not "shave" down to the white rind as it as it has a bitter taste. Yellow = mellow.

(K+) If you do not have a microplane, you can use a vegetable peeler. After peeling some strips off the lemon, use a knife to further chop the peel so that it is finely diced.

3 Add the parsley and lemon zest to the olive oil and stir in the minced garlic and salt. Cut the bread into 3/4 to 1-inch slices.

4 Brush one side with butter and spoon the gremolata onto the other side. I like a lot, but do it up your way.

5 Place the bread, buttered side down, on a hot grill. Heat over Medium-High for 2-3 mins to crisp the bottom and warm the gremolata. (Or place into a 385-degree oven for 5 mins. Keep an eye on it to make sure it doesn't burn because burnt toast is a bummer.)

(Tips) Slice the bread on the bias to make long, professional looking, diagonal slices.

VEGGIES... GROSS

I did not grow up to be big and strong. Well, technically, I never grew up; but maturity aside, vegetables are gross. I didn't spend my childhood, or any part of my life, bypassing red meat and seafood in favor of boiled broccoli or soggy, overcooked cauliflower. When I'm having a hard day at work and looking forward to a delicious dinner, it's not vegetables that I'm craving. But with age comes wisdom. And I now know the five secrets to cooking and enjoying vegetables:

#1 Don't overcook them.

#2 Grill, fry, or roast them — they don't all have to be boiled or steamed.

#3 Don't overcook them.

#4 Explore seasonings other than salt and pepper.

#5 Don't overcook them.

Tips Unless you have psychic powers, or still have a Magic 8-Ball from your childhood, cooking veggies to perfection is going to take some guesswork. But since most veggies are inexpensive, buy more than you need and practice to determine what temperatures and times work the best.

FIRE-CHARRED BROCCOLINI

If Chinese Cabbage and Broccoli had a baby... Trying to keep this book PG-13 so let's just call Broccolini the smaller, delicious version of broccoli. Because of its size, this cooks up quick in both a pan or on a grill.

Show Times:
broccolini
olive oil
pinch of both:
    coarse salt
    black pepper
lemon

1 Drizzle with olive oil and season with salt and pepper.

2 Let marinate while you get your grill heated up to Medium-High.

3 Grill directly over the flames for 3-4 minutes a side. Fire-kissed char is a good thing but if they catch on fire, probably time to move them off-heat for a bit.

4 Remove from the grill and then hit them with a squeeze from the lemon before serving.

GRILLED CARROTS

There are a variety of different spice options for grilling or oven roasting carrots. This isn't much of a recipe as there are only three ingredients – and one of them is carrots. But it's worth playing around with and developing your own "go-to" carrot dish as this is an easy and affordable side that can be thrown together at the last minute to compliment pretty much anything you're having for dinner. Bonus badassery if you serve them with the greens still attached for presentation points.

1 Wash or peel the carrots. Cut 1/4 to 1/2-inch off of each end and discard. If the carrots are thick (an inch or more diameter), you can slice them in half longways. This makes them easier to cook.

2 Drizzle with olive oil and then apply your seasonings. A simple one is just a few shakes of garlic-salt and a pinch of black pepper. Let them soak up the seasoning for as long as it takes to heat the grill or oven.

3 Grill over Medium-High Heat. Rotate 3-4 times throughout the cooking so that all of the sides get a chance to sit over the heat. Test for doneness by trying to bend the carrot in half. As soon as the carrot is soft enough to bend, remove from the heat. (They will continue cooking for a few mins when removed from the grill. So if you wait until they are completely soft before removing, then they will over-cook and be squishy-gross.)

GARLIC-PARM ZUCCHINI & SQUASH

Green & Gold. The two best colors for anyone from Wisconsin. What better way to class up a meal than by dropping some Championship hues on the plate? Zucchini and squash are affordable and cook up quick so they're an easy choice for a veggie side dish. But don't stop there, be a Pro Bowler and make garlic "bread" replacing the bread with the veggies. If you want me to eat my vegetables, adding melted cheese is certainly a strong and sound approach. Keeping the zucchini and squash intact (sliced lengthwise) is not only the easiest way to grill them up, but is also the best way to duplicate the look of garlic bread. Presentation is always worth the Extra Point Attempt.

Red-Zone Audibles:
1 zucchini
1 squash
1 Tbs unsalted butter
1/4 tsp garlic powder
1/4 tsp table salt
1/4 dried parsley
1/4 cup shredded mozzarella
1/8 cup shredded parmesan

1 Melt the butter and then stir in the garlic powder, salt, and parsley.

2 Cut a 1/2 inch off each end of the veggies then slice in half lengthwise. Use a fork to poke some holes down the flat side of each half.

3 Pour the garlic butter equally over all four pieces and let the sauce soak into the fork-holes. Top with the mozzarella cheese.

4 Grill (round side down) over Medium Heat (or bake at 385 degrees), for 5-6 mins. When done, finish by sprinkling the parmesan over the top.

XP: 110

SAUTÉED GARLIC MUSHROOMS

Fungi Friends:
1 lb of mushrooms, sliced
4 Tbs of unsalted butter
1 tsp minced garlic
1/4 tsp coarse ground salt
1/4 tsp black pepper

While these are a time-tested partner for steak, they are also good just on their own. Takes less than 10 minutes to bang these out so they're an easy side to make while waiting for your main course to cook up.

1 Heat the butter in a pan over Medium-Low Heat.

2 Add the garlic and brown for 2-3 minutes.

3 Season with the salt and pepper and stir through. Add the mushrooms and cook for 3-4 minutes until they absorb some of the garlic-butter sauce.

4 Remove from the heat while they are still firm – don't let them get soggy.

PICKLED ONIONS & RADISHES

I hate commercials. Not just because they interrupt my programming but because they are insulting. If the magic of television and film is the willful suspension of disbelief, advertisers are betting on us, the viewers, to be total morons (or too busy playing on our mobile devices to realize we're being insulted). —The beer commercials where they hike through the desert or mountain bike to the beach, yet their bottled beer is ice-cold when they reach their destination. —Commercials for health and beauty products, or dating apps, where every actor cast in the advertisement is flawless and has a face and body that you couldn't obtain with the world's best plastic surgeon. The worst are the commercials from pharmaceutical companies marketing their pills and injections by fear. *"Are you tired? Do you feel weak at the end of a long day? Have you ever had muscle soreness? It's not because you have to go to work and bust your ass in a thankless job, it's because you have scurvy. But with just 3 doses of Pickle Powder a day, you'll be on the path to recovery, happiness, and eternal enlightenment."*

I was going to expound on the virtues of pickled vegetables but now I'm worried that I might have scurvy. Thanks, big pharma!

Side Effects:
1 red onion or 12 radishes
1 cup white vinegar
1/2 cup water
1 tsp table salt
1/2 tsp sugar

1 Add the vinegar, water, salt, and sugar to a saucepan and warm over Medium Heat. Stir until the salt and sugar are dissolved. Once the brine starts to boil, turn off the heat.

2 Red Onion: Slice both ends off the onion and discard. Remove the skin and peel off the first layer of the onion and discard. Slice the onion in half lengthwise and then cut into thin slices.

Radishes: Cut the stem off each radish and then cut into slices.

3 Place the onions, the radishes, or both, in a sealable jar and pour the brine in. Make sure the vegetables are completely submerged in the brine. Screw on the lid and let the jar cool until it reaches room temp. Place in the fridge and let the brine work its magic for at least 24 hours (best after 3 days). Will keep up to a month.

Disclaimer: Eating pickled onions and radishes may cause excitability, maxi-flavoritis, enlarged taste-buds, acute yummy-yummies, chronic nom-noms, haunted bowel disease, Food Network Chef envy, delirium-deliciousness, the drools, finger-licking, and a case of 'you've-got-to-try-this'. If you have a smile that lasts for four or more hours, seek medical attention.

GERMAN RED CABBAGE

Mention "sauerkraut" and most people will tell you *"no thank you"*. But chances are their only experience with fermented cabbage was with something bought at the market and served out of a jar or can. Not only is homemade always better, but cabbage need not be of the sour variety. This traditional German cabbage dish is warm, sweet, and fantastic. Wunderbare!

Blaukraut:

7 cups sliced red cabbage
    (1 small cabbage)
1 ½ cups sliced green apple
    (1 Granny Smith)
1 ¼ cup sliced yellow onion
    (1/2 medium sized onion)
2 Tbs unsalted butter
1 tsp coarse ground salt
1/2 tsp black pepper
1/4 cup brown sugar
1/3 cup apple cider vinegar

1 Slice the cabbage in half through the core. Cut out the triangular core remaining in each half. Discard. Cut the cabbage into long, 1/4-inch strips.

2 Core the apple and cut into slices, and then cut across the slices and into 1/4-inch strips.

3 Peel the onion and discard the first layer. Chop in half. Cut the half into strips.

4 Heat a large pot over Medium-High Heat. Add the butter. When melted, add the onions, salt, and pepper. Sauté for 3-4 mins.

5 Add the green apple slices and stir together with the onions. Simmer for another 3-4 mins.

6 Whisk the brown sugar into the apple cider vinegar. Pour into the pot and then turn the Heat down to Low.

7 Add all of the cabbage and then stir everything together.

8 Cover and cook for 45-50 mins. After 30 mins, remove the lid and give everything a stir. If there is no more liquid in the pot, or the cabbage starts sticking to the bottom, add a 1/4 cup of water for the remainder of the cook time. Remove when the cabbage is tender (but not soggy).

CREAMY COOL-SLAW

Coleslaw is cabbage. Cabbage is a vegetable. Ya know how I feel about most vegetables. But shredded cabbage is redeemed by adding the nectar of the Gods, mayonnaise. Mayo fixes everything. Car out of gas, add mayo. Broke your leg, slather it in mayo. Don't have enough money for rent, mail your landlord an envelope full of mayo. This is a classic side dish with both BBQ and spicy food because it helps cut through the richness of smoked or grilled meat and the mayo-based sauce helps cool the fire of spicy wings or other hot-pepper based dishes.

Cabbage Collection:
1 Tbs sugar
1 tsp coarse ground salt
1/2 cup apple cider vinegar
3/4 cup mayo
2 Tbs sour cream
1 tsp black pepper
3 cups diced/sliced green cabbage
1 cup diced/sliced red cabbage
1 cup diced/sliced carrot
1/4 cup finely diced cilantro
1/4 cup finely diced green onions

1 Determine if you want your coleslaw in long, sliced strips, or chopped into diced chunks. It's the same ingredients, so it'll taste the same, but some folks are diehard Team Sliced while others root for Team Diced. Wars have been fought over less – so choose wisely.

2 In a large bowl, whisk the sugar and salt into the apple cider vinegar until it dissolves. Add the mayo, sour cream, and black pepper and whisk together until it is smooth.

3 Cut out the center core of the cabbage and discard. Dice, or slice, the leaves of the cabbage.

4 Peel the carrot and cut each end off. You can dice or slice, or use a grater to get the carrot down to size.

5 Chop the cilantro leaves and the green part of 1-2 green onions.

6 Add all of the veggies to the dressing and give them a toss through the happy sauce. Let sit in the fridge for at least an hour.

(K+) Check your local market for pre-packaged 'Coleslaw Mix'. This will save you some chopping time.

JOEY'S SMOKEY-SWEET GRILLED CORN

Here is a list of things my son is good at: Everything. He is one of those people that can just do it all. Ya know that TV Show 'MacGyver'? The one with the guy who disarms a bomb with a paperclip and stick of gum, hotwires a helicopter with a banana peel, and then rebuilds the engine of a Honda Accord with nothing but a Swiss Army Knife. Yep, Joey. When he's not out having adventures in his custom-built Jeep, he's sweating over his smoker and coming up with new ways to make me eat my vegetables.

• 2-3 ears of corn •

Jeep Accessories:
4 Tbs unsalted butter
1 Tbs smoked paprika
1/2 Tbs garlic powder
1/2 Tbs coarse ground salt

1 Pull back the husks but do not remove. Remove the silk strands that are between the husk and the corn and discard. Fold the husks back up.

2 Soak in a large pot of water (or fill your (clean) sink with water) for at least an hour.

3 Grill over Medium-High Heat for 20 mins rotating the corn every 5-6 mins so that all sides get kissed by the flames. (Alternatively you can roast these in the oven: 30 mins at 400 degrees.)

4 You can check for doneness by giving them a squeeze to make sure that the kernels are tender. When done, remove from the heat and let sit for 5 mins to cool slightly (and give you enough time to make the delicious smokey butter sauce).

5 Melt the butter in a small saucepan. Stir in the smoked paprika, garlic powder, and salt. Stir until it thickens into a buttery red paste.

6 When the corn is cool enough to handle, peel the husks back again, but don't remove them. You can wrap a husk around the base of the corn and tie your favorite Scout knot to turn the husks into a badass handle. Brush them with the smokey butter sauce.

THAI-STYLE CORN ON THE COB

Sweet, sour, spicy, salty. If you're able to hit all four of these flavors at once, then bottle it and pour it on everything. For a vegetable, I guess corn is pretty good. And if I'm going to eat corn, it's going to be grilled so I can get some texture on it. And if I'm going through the trouble of getting the grill rocking for a vegetable, then I'm going 4 for 4 on the flavor and working up this tasty Thai-Style sauce.

• 4-6 ears of corn •

The Four Flavors:
1-2 Tbs vegetable oil
1 shallot, finely diced
1 Tbs minced garlic
1 tsp of red curry paste
1 Tbs fish sauce
2 limes
1 tsp coarse ground salt
1 (15 oz) can of coconut milk
cilantro leaves (garnish)

1 Pull back the husks but do not remove. Remove the silk strands that are between the husk and the corn and discard. Fold the husks back up.

2 Soak in a large pot of water (or fill your (clean) sink with water) for at least an hour.

3 Grill over Medium-High Heat for 20 mins rotating the corn every 5-6 mins so that all sides get kissed by the flames. (Alternatively you can roast these in the oven. 30 mins at 400 degrees.)

4 Warm a large pan over Medium Heat. Add a couple Tbs of vegetable oil. Sauté the shallot and garlic for 4-5 mins, stirring to keep the garlic from burning.

5 Stir in the red curry paste. Add the fish sauce, the juice of 1 lime, and the coarse ground salt. Stir in the coconut milk. Simmer for 5-6 mins, stirring every minute or so to keep everything mingling in the coconut pool.

6 When the corn is cool enough to handle, peel the husks back again, without removing them (so you can use them as a handle). Spoon the coconut-lime sauce over the top and garnish with the cilantro and lime wedges.

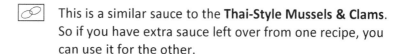 This is a similar sauce to the **Thai-Style Mussels & Clams**. So if you have extra sauce left over from one recipe, you can use it for the other.

DOUBLE BAKED POTATOES

Do you love baked potatoes? Do you love mashed potatoes? Is it possible to have both at the same time? I suck at math but even I know that 'Two for One' is a pretty good deal. Too bad this applies to potatoes and not buying Jameson or booking a flight to Alaska. Double Baked Potatoes are the brilliant combination of crispy skinned baked potatoes stuffed with creamy, cheesy, mashed potatoes. You don't need to be Katherine Johnson to know that the math adds up. This is a stellar dish, whether as a side or an entire meal. Double Baked Potatoes? It's a "Go".

Launch Status Check:

1 russet potato
(1 potato = 2 twice-baked
  potatoes)
olive oil
coarse ground salt
4 Tbs unsalted butter
1 Tbs sour cream
1/2 tsp garlic salt
1/4 tsp black pepper
1/4 cup shredded cheddar

HOW *NOT* TO BAKE A POTATO:
Avoid the following tuber myths.

Ø Do not wrap in aluminum foil
Ø Do not murder with a fork poking holes in the skin
Ø Do not open the oven to poke-check for doneness

SPUD-NIK LAUNCH SEQUENCE:

10 Preheat the oven to 400 degrees.

9 Rinse the potato in cold water to remove any dirt and then dry thoroughly with a dish towel or paper towel.

8 Coat in olive oil and sprinkle with coarse ground salt on all sides.

7 Place the potato right on the oven rack. Slide a sheet of aluminum foil or parchment paper on the rack below the potato to catch the olive oil drippings. Bake for 60 mins (70 mins if the potato is excessively large) without giving in to the temptation to open the oven to poke and prod (which only lets all the heat out).

6 After baking, remove the potato and check for doneness by inserting a small knife into the side of the potato. (Select the place on the potato where you will cut it in half. This leaves the "bottom" of each half intact and crispy.) They are done when the knife slides easily in and out and the insides are soft.

5 Slice in half lengthwise. Using a spoon, carefully scoop out the cooked potatoes without tearing the crispy skin. Place the scooped-out potatoes into a large bowl.

4 Add the unsalted butter, sour cream, garlic salt, and black pepper and work through until the butter is melted. If there are any chunks, use a fork to gently break them up. Fold in the shredded cheddar cheese.

(Tips) The less you handle the potatoes the creamier they will be. So try not to aggressively mix or overwork them.

3 Spoon the cheesy mixture back into the potato skins.

2 Turn the oven down to 385 degrees and place the two halves of the potato back in and cook for 10-12 minutes until the potato is rewarmed and the cheese melts.

1 Remove from the oven, garnish with another pinch of cheddar cheese and some chives or green onions.
The Eagle has landed.

(Tips) Bake 2 potatoes to double the amount of mashed potatoes you'll be able to pile into the two halves. Save the other (unused) halves for potato skin appetizers.

 Try adding bacon. Or replace the sour cream with **Ranch Dipping Sauce** or spinach-artichoke dip. Swap out the cheddar for smoked gouda or some blue cheese.

3-BEER GERMAN POTATO SALAD

Salad sucks. Unless it's warm. And has bacon. Let's check both those boxes at once and take this train to Octoberfest. Besides, since this isn't in the Salad Chapter, how can it really be a salad? Hmmm...

• 4 servings •

Bavarian Beer Bash:

3 bottles of German beer
3 potatoes (Yukon gold)
1/4 cup cooked bacon
  (3-4 slices)
1/2 cup diced red onion
1 Tbs flour
1 cup water
1/2 cup apple cider vinegar
1 ½ Tbs sugar
1 Tbs coarse ground salt
1/2 tsp black pepper
1/2 cup diced dill pickles

1 Cut the potatoes in half and place into a pot. Cover the potatoes in cold water and add some salt. Over Medium-High Heat, bring to a boil and cook until they are soft (15-20 mins of boiling).

Note:
Some prefer to peel the potatoes first. While I'm sure this makes a prettier potato salad, I don't mind the skins (and I'm too lazy to peel) so I usually leave them on.

2 While the potatoes are boiling, cook the bacon in a pan over Medium Heat (3-4 mins a side).

3 Drink one of the beers.

4 When the potatoes are done (a knife slides easily in and out), drain and set aside. When the bacon is cooked, remove from the pan and set aside to drain and cool.

5 If there is a lot of bacon grease, pour some out (but retain about 2 Tbs). Add the diced red onion to the bacon drippings and cook over Low Heat until they soften (4-5 mins).

6 Drink the 2nd beer.

7 After the onion is cooked, whisk in the flour and stir continually until it is broken down and mixed into the bacon drippings and onions without any lumps.

8 Combine the water and the apple cider vinegar. Mix the sugar, salt, and pepper, and whisk until the sugar dissolves. Pour into the pan and work it into the flour mixture. Turn the heat up to Medium.

9 Add the diced pickles and crumble the bacon into the pan. Stir all of the ingredients together and simmer until the sauce just begins to bubble (3-5 mins).

10 Slice the potatoes into 1/4-inch slices and add them. Flip the potatoes a few times to coat all of the slices in the sauce. Simmer over Low Heat for 8-10 mins, stirring often to give the potatoes an opportunity to absorb the sauce but not burn to the bottom of the pan. (If they start to stick, add a 1/4 cup of water.)

11 Serve with **Cream City Beer Brats**, **Bavarian Burgers**, and of course… with the 3rd beer.

HASSELBACK SCALLOPED POTATOES AU GRATIN

Buffalo Wing flavored Margaritas. Chicken Breast Tartare. Or my brother's favorite when he splurges and takes his wife out for a gourmet meal at The Gilded Truffle: Lobster stuffed with Tacos. Combining two tasty dishes does not always equate to a perfect marriage of flavors. But in this case... what could be better than the cheesy-goodness of au gratin potatoes, baked into the scalloped grooves of a crispy Hasselback Potato? Plus, this is one particularly pretty potato when perfectly plated and presented.

• 2 potatoes •

Potato Pairing:
2 Yukon gold potatoes
1 large shallot
2 Tbs unsalted butter
1/2 tsp garlic powder
1/4 tsp coarse ground salt
1/4 tsp black pepper
1 Tbs flour
1 cup milk
1 cup shredded cheddar

1 Preheat the oven to 400 degrees.

2 Place the potatoes directly on the rack and bake for 20 minutes.

3 While the potato is softening up, finely dice the shallot.

4 Melt the butter in a small saucepan over Low Heat. Add the shallots, garlic powder, and the salt and pepper. Cook the shallots down until they get soft (5 mins).

5 Whisk in the flour and continue to stir for 1-2 mins until the flour is absorbed by the butter.

6 Whisk in the milk. Cook, stirring occasionally, until the milk warms and just starts to bubble (about 5 mins).

7 Add the cheese in small handfuls, while whisking continually until it melts. After it is creamy, add another handful. Repeat until all the cheese is melted into the sauce. Turn off the heat.

8 After the potatoes are par-cooked, remove from the oven and lay them on a cutting board. I prefer to peel them at this point but you can just as easily leave the skin on. Place a wooden spoon (or other narrow utensil or object) on each side of the potato. Starting at one end of the potato, slide the knife down to whatever utensil or object you have placed on each side (to prevent you from cutting all the way through). The wooden spoons are your guide to help you keep the potato intact as you continue to make slices 1/8-inch apart down the length of the potato.

9 Place the potatoes in a small casserole dish (or oven safe bowl) and spoon the cheese mixture over the top. Really work the cheese sauce down into and between each sliced segment. Don't be shy. We're all friends here.

10 Place the potatoes back into the 400-degree oven and cook for another 20 mins.

11 When the potatoes have softened and the cheese is baked up, carefully remove them so that they remain intact. Serve as, or with, your meal.

 If you have some cheese remaining, you can also spoon some of the cheese sauce over the top prior to serving to make them extra cheesy.

 Buy whole cheese and shred it yourself. While this is not only more economical, pre-shredded packaged cheese does not melt as well into the desired creamy-smooth consistency.

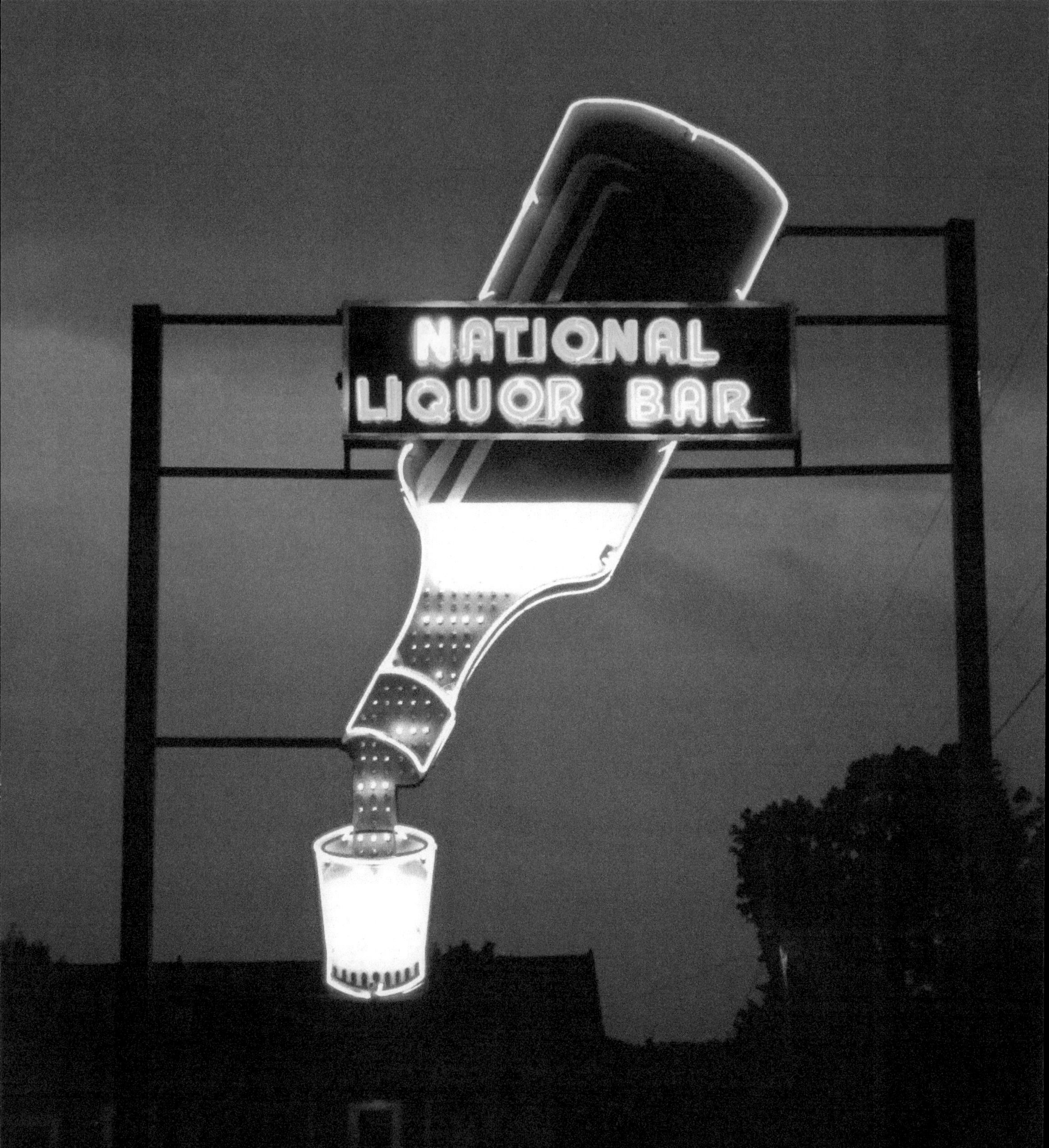
NATIONAL
LIQUOR BAR

HOMEMADE SPICE BLENDS

It's time to go beyond table salt and black pepper. Step past sea salt and white pepper. Get online and order yourself some Smoked Volcanic Salt and a jar of Aleppo Pepper. If you want to next-level your cook game, be fearless when you start building your spice shelf, or cabinet, or entire closet. Try different spices, and combinations of spices, to develop and expand your palate. When you're ready, then it's time to create your own spice blends.

1 Each time you go to the store, or every time you try a new recipe, buy a new spice. Build your collection over time, little by little. Ordering dry spices in bulk from the inter-web is also an affordable way to load up on the spices you use the most.

2 Keep your eye out for super-cool glass jars or bottles. Remove any labels or stickers, wash them thoroughly, and save them for a rainy day when you feel like developing your own spice blend.

3 Taste and try, and re-taste and re-try, all of the different spices. Everyone has a different palate. Try to find a spice you enjoy in each flavor category: salty, sweet, savory, spicy.

4 Combine a small amount of the different spices. Add more or less of each one until you like the balance of the blend. Keep a written log as you experiment so that you can keep track of how much of each spice you land on.

5 Keeping the ratio intact, you're now ready to mix up a large enough batch to fill your super-cool jar or bottle.

6 Come up with a unique and personalized name for your homemade spice blend, dry rub, or seasoning. Here's some badass examples to get you started:

The Mountain Man's Moose Mix

Atomic Radiation Kill Zone Spice Blend

. 50 Cal Tracer Rib Rub

~~Happy Unicorn Puppy Rainbow Rub~~

Scorpion Hurricane Napalm Spice Blast

⚠ If you really want to be a culinary cowgirl or kitchen cowboy, bypass the small glass and plastic spice shakers and work up a large batch of your custom blend and keep it in a liquor bottle. Serving your family-recipe rib rub in a bourbon jug, or giving your secret fry seasoning in a tequila bottle as a gift, is the very definition of Badass Cookery.

42.878185, -88.303247

SALT

One of the earliest references to salt came from an area near Shandong China. The Dawenkou culture was evaporating brine into salt over 6,000 years ago.

A Chinese pharmacological text from 4,700 years ago, the Png-tzao-kan-mu, recorded more than 40 different types of salt.

In ancient times, salt was more valuable than gold because it was used to preserve food. This was vital during the harsh winters when people had to rely on their food stores to survive prior to the invention of the icebox and refrigerators.

When Alexander the Great led his army East across Asia, they inadvertently discovered one of the World's largest underground rock salt deposits. While resting in Khewra (in modern day Pakistan), the soldiers noticed that their horses were licking rocks. They soon realized that these "rocks" were large rock salt crystals.

Whether fact or myth, some believe that Roman soldiers were paid in salt. In Latin, "sal dare" means "to give salt". Combining these words, "sal" and "dar" may be where the word "soldier" comes from. The word "salary" may also be based on this payment they received.

One of the first great Roman roads was the Via Salaria. Which means "salt road".

We only eat 6% of all of the salt produced in the World. The rest is used in manufacturing and for other uses (like de-salting our icy roadways in winter).

The human body needs salt to survive. Hyponatremia is a condition where the salt in your blood can drop to fatal levels. This can happen if you drink too much water. (Like a lot of water – A LOT, so don't be concerned if you're hydrating regularly).

Salar de Uyuni is the World's largest salt flat covering almost 4,000 square miles. (The State of Delaware and two Rhode Islands would fit within the borders of this playa.) It is in southwest Bolivia and is at an altitude of almost 12,000 feet above sea level. If you are a Star Wars fan, this salt flat was where they shot the battle sequence on the Planet Crait in the movie 'Star Wars: The Last Jedi'.

Salt is mainly the mineral sodium chloride (NaCl). There is a salt that is used in the manufacture of certain types of cheese to help it melt and stay creamy. The chemical formula for this salt happens to be NaCHO.

Mined salts can take on the color of the other minerals present in the location they are mined from. Some common colored, mineral salts are: Persian Blue Diamond Salt, Black Lava Salt, Hawaiian Alaea Red Salt, Himalayan Black Salt, and the currently popular, Pink Salt.

The Palacio de Sal is a hotel made out of salt bricks. In addition to the floors and walls of the hotel, the tables, chairs, and beds, are all made of salt. As water dissolves salt, this hotel has to be constantly maintained and repaired when it rains.

Sea Salts are not mined but instead come from evaporated sea water. These salts are considered a higher quality than mined salts as the region, and type of water, where the salt is collected imparts different flavors and unique shapes of the crystals.

One of the most expensive and unique salts in the World is called "Amethyst Bamboo 9x". It is a Korean sea salt which is sealed into a length of bamboo and then placed into a roaring hot, wood furnace. The salt is heated and cooled eight times. The ninth time it is heated, the fire is stoked to almost 1,500 degrees which melts the salt into a thick liquid (like lava). It is then poured out and allowed to cool and solidify back into super-condensed, and flavor packed, crystals.

THE WORLD'S WORST FOOD

Is it 'Ketchup' or 'Catsup'? Who cares. High fructose corn syrup and tomato paste? Ugh. I'd rather drink the juice out of a can of tuna – after it's been sitting on the dashboard of my car – in Phoenix – in July. Too much? Don't take my word for it. Consider the impact that this horrendous condiment has had on the history of our country:

 1587
British colonists must leave their settlement in Roanoke when they run out of Ketchup. When Governor John White returns from England three years later, he finds the settlement abandoned and all of the colonists missing. The only clue as to what might have happened was a single word scratched into a tree: "Croatoan" – an Algonquian Indian word for "should have used Mustard".

 1692
A young resident of Massachusetts dips her French Fries into delicious Ranch Dressing. The trend catches on with several young girls in the town of Salem. The Puritanical town leaders are horrified by this unnatural adnomination of nature and accuse the girls of being witches. They are arrested, tried, and executed for not using the one and only approved condiment of the time, Ketchup.

 December 16, 1773
In protest of the Condiment Act of 1773, the Sons of Liberty raid a ship from the British East India Company that was importing Ketchup. Since the colonists were being taxed on this tomatoey-paste, even though they were not represented in Parliament, they threw all of the bottles into Boston Harbor. This was one of the catalysts of the American War of Independence.

 January, 1847
George Donner leads a wagon-train of pioneers across the snow-covered mountains into California. Snowed in by the brutal Sierra Nevada winter, they are forced to take shelter and wait for Spring. With their supplies running low, all they have to eat are a collection of small Ketchup packets left over from the last drive-thru they ate lunch at. With their only choice of food Ketchup or each other, several in the party refuse to eat the Ketchup and instead resort to cannibalism to survive.

 April 12, 1861
Confederate Forces fire upon Fort Sumpter in South Carolina when Union Troops are observed putting Ketchup on their brats. This event is widely regarded as the first armed conflict of the American Civil War.

 October 8, 1871
In a small barn on DeKoven Street, Mrs. O'Leary tries to feed her cow Ketchup. Rejecting the ridiculous condiment, the cow attempts to escape and inadvertently kicks over a gas lamp which ignites the barn. Strong winds then spread the fire across Chicago burning much of the city to the ground. This same evening, another fire starts in Peshtigo Wisconsin and spreads across the state and into Michigan. While this fire was significantly larger than the one in Chicago, and would become the deadliest fire in American History, it wasn't reported on any of the national cable news networks as it had nothing to do with Ketchup and was thus labeled "fake news".

September 6, 1901

The Pan-American Exposition is held in Buffalo New York. Spectators from all over the World attend to sample the city's namesake: spicy chicken wings. President McKinley presides over the Expo and samples the various items being exhibited. After dipping a chicken wing into Ketchup instead of Blue Cheese Dressing, he is shot by a bystander and succumbs to his wounds the following week. The assassination would be blamed on an anarchist but conspiracy theorists have long blamed the condiment.

October 1929

Investors over-speculate on the value of Ketchup. When these stocks are rapidly sold off, the value of this condiment-commodity plummets, taking Wall Street with it. The over-reliance and misplaced popularity of this tomato-based product led to the Great Depression of the 1930s.

May 6, 1937

The passenger airship LZ 129, named "Hindenburg", journeys from Germany to New Jersey. After flying through inclement weather, it attempts to land at a Naval Air Station in Lakehurst. Due to the rain, static electricity ignites the high fructose corn syrup, a primary ingredient in Ketchup, and the zeppelin bursts into flames and crashes. Ketchup is soon discontinued as a fuel for airships. Passenger airplanes replace the popularity of the flying blimps and mustard starts appearing on hotdogs.

September 25, 1959

Soviet leader Nikita Khrushchev meets with President Eisenhower at Camp David to discuss nuclear disarmament. When dinner is served, the two leaders argue over whether Ketchup is better than Mustard. Khrushchev protests by removing his shoe and banging it on the table. Two years later, Khrushchev starts building a wall in Berlin to keep Western influence and tomato-based condiments out of the Soviet Bloc. The United States and the Soviet Union then enter a Cold War for the next three decades.

March 28, 1979

Reactor #2 in the Three Mile Island Nuclear Generating Station overheats when the Ketchup in the cooling tanks congeals and the sticky paste causes a valve to get stuck. Radioactive material then overwhelms the reactor causing a meltdown. It takes 14 years to clean up the radioactive Ketchup.

December 31, 1999

After years of referring to sweetened tomato paste as either "Ketchup" or "Catsup" a massive, global effort was undertaken to consolidate the multiple names for this sauce into a single, recognized, condiment. "Y2K", as it was called, would align all of the names to "Ketchup" on January 1st, 2000. A general panic spread among the populace who believed that the new millennium would crash computers, the economy, and our way of life in general. This led to the increased popularity of honey-mustard, Siracha, aioli, and other flavored mayonnaises (which continues to this very day).

XP CHART
(log your experience points and level up)

APPS

French Onion Soup Sliders	☐ 200
Festival Fare Mozz Sticks	☐ 100
49er Brie & Bread	☐ 80
Rockin' Rumaki	☐ 40
Siracha Deviled Eggs	☐ 60
BONUS *XP*: Peeling all eggs perfectly	☐ +100
Aunt Jo's Holiday Shrimp Dip	☐ 50
BONUS *XP*: Making it for a holiday or birthday	☐ +10
Grandma Leonardelli's Oliva Schiacciate	☐ 100
BONUS *XP*: Crushing the olives with a glass soda bottle	☐ +10
68th Street Fried Eggplant	☐ 120
Snack Time	☐ 75
Chapter Bonus (completed all recipes)	☐ +100

SALAD

Greek Salad	☐ 50
Rogue Squadron Salad Bites	☐ 80
BONUS *XP*: Making it while watching any of the Star Wars movies	☐ +10
Caprese Salad	☐ 50
Antipasto Pasta Salad	☐ 120
Market Deli Seafood Salad	☐ 50
Orzo Pasta Salad	☐ 110
BONUS *XP*: Serving it in a hollowed-out vegetable	☐ +10
Hawaiian Mac Salad	☐ 115
Chapter Bonus (completed all recipes)	☐ +85

CHICKEN

Poutine Chicken Sandwich	☐ 150
BONUS *XP*: If you know all the words to Rush's song 'YYZ'	☐ -50
BONUS *XP*: If you caught the trickery above	☐ +50
Kevin's Chicken	☐ 165
Ti-Malice Haitian Hot Sauce	☐ 90
BONUS *XP*: Keeping it in a cool-ass bottle	☐ +5
TLC Chicken Piccata	☐ 180
Tina's Char Siu Chicken	☐ 150
The World's Best Chinese BBQ Tacos	☐ 185
Chapter Bonus (completed all recipes)	☐ +150

WINGS

Bison Wings	☐ 120
Pelican Wings	☐ 115
BONUS *XP*: Making a Mint Julip	☐ +20
Chinese Salt & Pepper Wings	☐ 120
Balrog Fire Wings	☐ 200
Nashville Scored Chicken	☐ 140
BONUS *XP*: Making the hottest ones, listening to The Doors 'The End'	☐ +25
Code-7 Smoked Wings	☐ 250
Alabama BBQ Sauce	☐ 40
BONUS *XP*: Making the King's Original Hawaiian Rolls Garlic Bread	☐ +20
Blue Cheese Dressing	☐ 50
Ranch Dipping Sauce	☐ 50
Chapter Bonus (completed all recipes)	☐ +150

PORK

Cream City Beer Brats	☐ 80
BONUS *XP*: Making it with the suggested beer	☐ +20
Jalapeno Relish	☐ 50
Bavarian Beaver Burger	☐ 100
Mr. Drek's AKA Pizza	☐ 120
BONUS *XP*: Defeating a supervillain's plot to overthrow the world	☐ +1000
South Street Seared Chops	☐ 160
Cilantro-Lime Rice	☐ 80
Cajun Smothered Chops	☐ 200
The Heartbreaker	☐ 170
Chapter Bonus (completed all recipes)	☐ +150

BURGERS

Brewski Burger	☐ 150
Box Alarm Burger	☐ 140
Beer-Butter Onions	☐ 30
Deadwood Burger	☐ 120
BONUS *XP*: Rocking the bacon-weave	☐ +20
Haole Sliders	☐ 125
Chapter Bonus (completed all recipes)	☐ +120

STEAK N' BEEF

Pan Seared Steak	☐ 140
The Sandwich of Brotherly Love	☐ 100
Grilled Flat Iron Steak	☐ 120
BONUS *XP*: Grilling in the rain	☐ +1
BONUS *XP*: Grilling in the snow	☐ +3
Chimichurri	☐ 50
Burgundy Mushroom Sauce	☐ 100
Campfire Steak	☐ 120
BONUS *XP*: Making it over a wood burning fire	☐ +50
Bulgogi Short Ribs	☐ 100
Chapter Bonus (completed all recipes)	☐ +120

TACOS

Teri's Tacos	☐ 120
Taco Truck Quesadillas	☐ 65
Aztec Avocado Sauce	☐ 50
Grilled Citrus Shrimp Tacos	☐ 125
Crema-verde Dipping Sauce	☐ 30
Green Onion Aioli	☐ 60
Tomatillo Salsa Verde	☐ 90
BONUS *XP*: Extra points if you know the acronym 'PSAP'	☐ +25
Mexican Cabbage Salsa	☐ 45
Curtido	☐ 50
Chapter Bonus (completed all recipes)	☐ +80

SHRIMP

Naked Shrimp	☐ 100
BONUS *XP*: Making the homemade Shrimp Cocktail Sauce	☐ +10
29 Razor Remoulade	☐ 125
BONUS *XP*: Making it for a Packer's Game	☐ +10
BONUS *XP*: If it's a Playoff Game	☐ +20
BONUS *XP*: If the Pack is in the Big Game	☐ +50
NOLA BBQ Shrimp	☐ 190
Boom-Stick Buffalo Shrimp	☐ 135
BONUS *XP*: Making it with Bruce Campbell	☐ +1000
BONUS *XP*: You are Bruce Campbell	☐ +100,000
Shrimp Two-O-Nine	☐ 135
Mango-Habanero Shrimp Skewers	☐ 200
BONUS *XP*: Pairing it with a Carlton Draught or VB	☐ +50
Chapter Bonus (completed all recipes)	☐ +150

SEAFOOD

Wild Salmon with Leek Cream Sauce	☐ 150
San Fran Beer Clams	☐ 120
BONUS *XP*: Making it with Anchor Steam Beer	☐ +20
QA Wine Mussels	☐ 110
BONUS *XP*: If you work, or have worked, in Quality Management	☐ +25
Thai-Style Mussels & Clams	☐ 200
Grilled Octopus	☐ 120
Octopus Salad	☐ 140
Chapter Bonus (completed all recipes)	☐ +150

PASTA

Mom's Stuffed Conchiglie	☐ 160
BONUS *XP*: Making heart shaped garlic bread	☐ +20
Shrimp "I know it was you" Alfredo	☐ 140
Baked Rigatoni-Soprano	☐ 200
BONUS *XP*: Going for dessert at Holsten's in Bloomfield	☐ +500
Prostitute Pasta	☐ 125
BONUS *XP*: Rockin' to Track #3 on the Album 'Outlandos d'Amour'	☐ +20
Gremolata Bread	☐ 100
Chapter Bonus (completed all recipes)	☐ +145

VEGGIES...GROSS

Fire-Charred Broccolini	☐ 50
Grilled Carrots	☐ 50
Garlic-Parm Zucchini & Squash	☐ 55
Sautéed Garlic Mushrooms	☐ 60
Pickled Onions & Radishes	☐ 45
Creamy Cool-Slaw	☐ 50
Joey's Smokey-Sweet Grilled Corn	☐ 55
Thai-Style Corn on the Cob	☐ 95
Double Baked Potatoes	☐ 100
BONUS *XP*: Making double-stuffed	☐ +20
3-Beer German Potato Salad	☐ 150
BONUS *XP*: If Hacker-Pschorr Weiss is your beer of choice	☐ +20
Hasselback Scalloped Potatoes Au Gratin	☐ 200
German Red Cabbage	☐ 110
Chapter Bonus (completed all recipes)	☐ +85

SPICES

Making your own homemade Spice Blend	☐ 50
BONUS *XP*: Putting it in a cool-ass bottle	☐ 20

OVERALL BONUS *XP*

Getting all of the stupid references and quotes in the recipes	☐ 50,000
Defeating a Demogorgon	☐ 100,000
Making the Ice Recipe	☐ 250,000

LEVEL UP

XP	LEVEL	BRIGADE HIERARCHY
250	Level 1	Take-Out & Delivery Specialist
500	Level 2	Corporal Cup-O-Noodle
800	Level 3	Toaster Oven Arsonist
1,200	Level 4	Master of Aloe & Band-Aids
1,700	Level 5	Cooking Channel Neophyte
2,350	Level 6	Weekend Warrior
3,100	Level 7	Pot-Luck Pro
4,000	Level 8	Carbonite-Inspired Delusions of Grandeur
5,000	Level 9	Classically Trained Chef – In Mediocracy
6,500	Level 10	Prep Padawan
8,000	Level 11	Super Sous Chef
10,000	Level 12	Protein Pro-Bowler
11,180	Level 13	Chancellor of Cookery
11,764	Level 14	Admiral of the USS Kitchen
411,764	Level 15	Baron Von Badassery

🔗 INGREDIENTS INDEX

Leftovers. Gross. The word itself conjures images of repurposed chili or the 4th day of Sloppy Joes. But that is only the perception of the unimaginative. It's culinary connotation. Consider it a reno. Flip through your television or streaming content and you'll no doubt find a half dozen shows dedicated to flipping, or renovating, old properties. Positioned in this way, building up leftovers into a different recipe is delicious, convenient, and economical. You can use the index below to cross-reference recipes with whatever you find in your fridge or pantry.

CHARACTER SHEET

CLASS: Author

LEVEL: 16

ALIGNMENT: Chaotic Good

STRENGTH	DEXTERITY	CONSTITUTION
8	11	12

INTELLIGENCE	WISDOM	CHARISMA
18	15	16

ACKNOWLEDGMENTS:

The concept for this book was conceived in a hospital, bedside, as I worried and waited for my wife to recover and be discharged. I tend to over-focus on things – and usually the wrong things. The stress of my job, frustrations of the day, getting stuck in traffic and having your morning coffee made incorrectly; pale in comparison to worrying about my best friend and wife. I feel guilty that it took such a significant event for me to reprioritize what is truly important in life – family. This book, a collection of memories, photos, and familiar recipes, is a love letter to my family. It was written for them. (Too cheesy for you? Then buy some wine and crackers for the perfect pairing.)

www.BadassCookery.com

BIO:

Kevin was born and raised in the frozen tundra of the Badger State and grew up sucking at sports but rocking it out as an above average Dungeon Master. After completing the Kessel Run in less than 11 parsecs (a galactic record) he was named the 10th member of the Fellowship at the Council of Elrond. On his way to Mordor, he took a wrong turn in King's Landing and wound up in New Orleans where he refined his cook skills, got into the right kind of trouble, and in general, tried to avoid growing up. When that inevitable day came, and it was time to start adulting, he settled in California and spent the majority of his professional life working in Emergency Dispatch. After a couple decades under the headset in one of the world's most stressful jobs, it was time to get back to the things he enjoyed: travel, photography, writing, annoying people by quoting lines from his favorite movies, and cooking. While not the brightest bulb in the chandelier, Kevin realized that the Venn Diagram of his interests all intersected at writing a cookbook. His juvenile obsession with obscure references brings a unique approach to the genre while sharing easy and delicious recipes.

CPSIA information can be obtained
at www.ICGtesting.com
Printed in the USA
BVHW021309151221
624120BV00016B/682